# Sanderson

# *The Essence of English Decoration*

MARY SCHOESER

# Sanderson
# *The Essence of English Decoration*

*With 239 illustrations, 228 in colour*

Thames & Hudson

To Terry, for still being here

TITLE PAGE

'Eglantine', a screen-printed glazed cotton designed in 1957 in the Parisian
Pollet studio, was in the Sanderson range from 1962 until 1972. It was
reissued in the Sanderson 150th Anniversary collection in spring 2010.

First published in the United Kingdom in 2010 by Thames & Hudson Ltd,
181A High Holborn, London WC1V 7QX

thamesandhudson.com

British Library Cataloguing-in-Publication Data
A catalogue record for this book is available from the British Library

ISBN 978-0-500-51519-8

Printed and bound in China by C&C Offset Printing Co. Ltd.

# Preface

## ZANDRA RHODES

My reacquaintance with Sanderson started when Mary Schoeser contacted me to identify the Sanderson Palladio wallpaper that I designed in the early 1960s. It brought back so many memories of my college days in the late 1950s and early 60s, and of the pride and honour one felt in selling Palladio designs to Sanderson.

As a student at Medway College of Art, I was taught by Barbara Brown, the dramatic and exotic personality who first put textiles in my blood. Barbara arranged for me and two other students to visit Manchester, then the capital of the British textile and wallpaper industry. Seeing factories doing silk-screening, block-printing and fabric dyeing was a wonderful experience, but most of the designs were depressingly awful. Manchester was smoky, with chimneys and 'dark Satanic mills' like in a Lowry painting, *and* raining all the time! Shining against all this dross were the Palladio wallpapers in the showrooms: 'Treescape' by Audrey Levy or her 'Phantom Rose' with its large, bold, sketchy roses, and Marino Marini's 'Horses' side-by-side with 'Sicilian Lion' by Robert Nicholson. These papers were also in all the best architectural magazines.

The 1950s had been austere, but throughout the decade a new era of great British interior design was already in its formative stages. Lucienne Day was part of the new vernacular, followed by innovative designers such as Barbara Brown, and others who were part of the Heal's empire. Then, in 1960, Sanderson remodelled its showrooms in Berners Street. These were the finest in the UK: there were twenty-eight room settings that the public were *allowed* to visit and see (although they could still only buy Sanderson products through their decorators!) Beautiful modern fabrics were available from three main sources at the time – Heal's, Liberty and Sanderson – but in Sanderson's very visible showrooms, Palladio wallpaper made the firm the cutting-edge leader. High standards of production, as well as the dramatic Palladio repeat sizes, raised Sanderson above the rest of the industry and gave the brand an identifiable 'face' that the world could recognise and admire.

All the great British textile designers passed through, if not the Heal's empire, the Sanderson Palladio 'school'. My heady days at the Royal College of Art from 1960 to 1963 were spent alongside many of the designers who were commissioned to create patterns for the Palladio range. Howard Carter was one year ahead of me and Peter Hall was a senior, creating his textured stripes with Roger Nicholson, who was Professor of Textiles at the RCA. Their papers were key decorative statements for the iconic Royal Garden Hotel, which was then being built in Kensington. With the foundation of Palladio collections a golden age of wallpaper had begun, and these designs represented all that we had been taught to aspire to.

Although the excitement I felt for dress textiles, which I had not yet explored in the early 1960s, would soon lead me to different pastures, I was thrilled when I finally had the opportunity to contribute to a Sanderson Palladio collection. I am just as delighted now to learn how often innovation has been part of the Sanderson history, as readers of this fascinating book will discover for themselves.

*Opposite* A detail from 'Zandra', designed in the early 1960s by Zandra Rhodes and included in the influential 1968 wallpaper collection, Palladio 8. Produced in Sanderson's Perivale factory, it contained the first screen-printed vinyl wallcoverings issued by any branch of the Wallpaper Manufacturers' Association (WPM).

*Overleaf* A Sanderson advertisement designed by Horace Taylor, 1930–34.

SANDERSON
SUNTESTED
WALLPAPERS

# Introduction

CHRISTINE WOODS

*Curator (Wallpapers)*
*The Whitworth Art Gallery, University of Manchester*

I n common with many other children born in the post-Second World War period, I grew up with Sanderson wallpapers. They provided the backdrop to my teenage life. An ivy trail graced the walls of the hall of my parents' 1930s suburban semi and later, after a brief romance with the ubiquitous woodchip, my father hung a floral stripe (based on an eighteenth-century textile pattern) in the master bedroom. The 'feature wall' in the dining room still looks fresh more than thirty years after its installation.

In the mid-1980s I came to know the company more intimately when I became its archivist and participated in the celebration of its 125th anniversary. Witnessing Sanderson's growing reputation for chintz and country-house style, I wondered whether it would become a blessing or a curse for the firm. As it turned out, it was to become a distinct part of the Sanderson offerings, but this did not prevent the company from continuing to adapt to new trends.

Sanderson began as an agent and importer of expensive French wallpapers. This is not surprising. A lack of confidence in home-grown design led nineteenth-century British wallpaper manufacturers, although critical of their French counterparts, to spend much time and money buying or copying what were then seen as more fashionable and polished French patterns. But by the time of Arthur Sanderson's death in 1882, widespread acceptance of mechanisation and a rising middle class had encouraged dramatic growth in the market for wallpapers and his firm was manufacturing its own ranges. Indeed, it ranked among the major wallpaper manufacturers in London. The fashion for all things French had waned and, taking advantage of the new confidence in British design, the firm was employing accomplished and well-known English freelancers as well as its own studio artists to produce its designs.

By 1884 Sanderson's three sons had embarked on an ambitious programme of expansion, acquiring new premises, several other well-known firms and, of equal importance, these firms' patterns – material that forms the basis of one of the most important design archives in the world and underpins much of the Sanderson product today. In a market once saturated with wallpapers, the Sanderson brothers' entrepreneurial flair enabled the firm to maintain a prime position.

Continuing to retain its independence while sheltering under the umbrella of a joint-stock company (the Wallpaper Manufacturers Limited, or 'WPM'), by 1920 the firm had won medals at several international exhibitions, operated one of the finest showrooms in London, and was supplying paint and other necessaries to the decorating trade. It had sole agencies for numerous foreign firms, whose products were shown the length and breadth of England by travelling salesmen equipped with specially made portable pattern books. Its own wallpapers were becoming popular in export markets worldwide. In retrospect, it seems almost inevitable that the Sandersons' next venture would focus on production of printed textiles, but it is unlikely that the family could have foreseen the radical change that this project would bring to the firm's image. Nor could they have anticipated that the move into textiles would contribute to the company's survival after the Second World War, when paper supplies were restricted and consumers were turning to paint for decorative salvation after years of deprivation and gloom.

When Arthur Sanderson established his business in 1860, at the age of thirty-one, he could not have imagined that a century later it would have grown into a company with a landmark London showroom, serving an international market with a network of agencies worldwide and a name that was known, in the UK certainly, in almost every household. Fifty years further on, I can state with some certainty that Sanderson's survival of the numerous take-overs and mergers of the late twentieth century is nothing short of a miracle.

This book charts that Sanderson story, and in doing so provides a glimpse of the history of the British domestic furnishings industry, of wallpaper in particular. It also highlights the impact individual personalities have had on the firm, how they have responded to changing social and economic circumstances, and how their products have been marketed and consumed.

Sanderson changed my life: it was there that I became hooked on wallpaper. I have never looked back and am delighted to see that Sanderson is also looking to the future.

# *The Business Begins*

¶ In 1860 Arthur Sanderson establishes himself in Islington, London, as an importer of French wallpapers.

¶ His merchandise features expensive, luxurious wallpapers, such as the panoramic and imitation-leather papers manufactured by Paul Balin of Paris, for whom Sanderson is the sole agent in England.

¶ He moves to Soho Square in central London in 1861 or 1862 and is soon becoming known as one of the largest dealers in foreign goods in England.

¶ In 1865 Sanderson moves to nearby Berners Street; the firm's showroom remains there until 1992.

¶ In 1868 Charles L. Eastlake publishes his *Hints on Household Taste*, which becomes one of the era's most influential volumes on all aspects of the domestic interior and promotes the division of walls into dado, filling and frieze while decrying overly ornate decoration.

¶ Arthur Sanderson begins having designs commission-printed by block-printers in England in 1868 or 1869.

¶ Sanderson's oldest son, John, joins the firm in 1877.

¶ In 1879 Sanderson acquires land at Chiswick and builds a wallpaper factory.

In 1860 Arthur Sanderson founded the Sanderson firm in London as an importer of French wallpapers. From these modest beginnings the company would develop into one of England's leading manufacturers of decorative products, famous not only for its own wallpapers, but also for its textiles, paints and decorative objects.

Aged thirty-one at the time, Arthur Sanderson was apparently no stranger to the business of wallpapering, having had 'a training in several of the leading houses in the trade', although the precise details of his early career are not known.[1] The 1860 edition of the London Post Office's *Trades Directory*, which records Sanderson's location as 24 Upper Street in Islington, lists no fewer than 168 other paperhangers and paperhanging manufacturers operating in the city at the time. One might imagine that Sanderson had some acquaintence with – and perhaps even trained at – the manufactories of Holmes & Aubert, Ridley & Whitley and Carlisle & Clegg, all of which were then also located in Islington. However, the only certainty in Sanderson's background is that just prior to establishing his own firm, he had been in partnership with one Ward, probably a relative of his first wife, Jane Ward, whom he married in the late 1850s. An advertisement from this period describes Sanderson & Ward as purveyors of stationery (both wholesale and retail), musical scores and 'Fancy Goods in great variety'. The provision of this combination of products, together with wallpaper and other printed items such as illustrated notices or posters, was not unusual for businesses at the time; a similar range was offered by Jeffrey, Wise & Co. in Whitechapel, which in 1864, as Jeffrey & Co., dedicated itself to wallpaper manufacture alone. Arthur Sanderson's firm would follow a similar trajectory.

Sanderson soon moved his family and business a mile south to either 17 or 19 Soho Square, where buildings that had once housed aristocrats and ambassadors were becoming home to commercial enterprises such as the condiment makers Crosse & Blackwell. Here he displayed the wares of several French wallpaper manufacturers, among them Bezault & Pattey *fils*, Paul Balin, and Zuber & Cie.[2] Other firms in Sanderson's repertoire may have included Defosse & Karth and L. Danois (called Riquiez & Danois from 1866–73 and Danois thereafter).[3] All produced expensive papers, including picturesque panoramic panels, chintz and imitation leathers. These exclusive imported wares formed the early foundation of Sanderson's business.

Wallpapers with the three-dimensionality of textiles and stamped leathers became a speciality of Paul Balin, a designer who purchased the Parisian factory of Genoux & Bader in 1863. From these premises, located at 236 rue du Faubourg Saint-Antoine, Balin perfected a process that made it possible to emboss papers cold, using a *balancier*, or fly-press, although some historians claim the method had been invented years earlier by A. Saegers, and the date of Balin's patent for the process is variously recorded as 1863 and 1866–69.[4] But the unrivalled perfection of Balin's papers – imitating Cordovan leather and historic textiles – was indisputable. His products were labour-intensive to produce and retailed at extremely high prices for the time, costing as much as ten gold francs per metre, whereas those of his predecessors had cost only a few francs for an entire roll.[5] After winning a medal at the 1867 Exposition Universelle in Paris, his papers were imitated by other manufacturers, including Zuber.[6] In 1873 Balin received a prize at the Vienna

*Previous page* Arthur Sanderson began his business selling luxurious French papers such as this embossed example imported from Paul Balin of Paris.

*Top* Arthur Sanderson photographed *c*. 1878, when he was near the age of fifty.

*Above* From about 1861 to 1865, Arthur Sanderson ran his business and lived with his family in the south-west corner of Soho Square, here illustrated in J. B. Papworth's *Select Views of London* (1816).

*Above left* Balin's embossed leather papers ranged in style from tile-like patterns, often placed in dining rooms and hallways, to elaborate designs destined for drawing rooms.

*Above right* This block-printed frieze, in the lush floral style typical of French papers imported

by Sanderson during the 1860s, may have been printed by the Parisian firm Bezault & Pattey *fils*.

*Below* Hand block-printed pictorial friezes, such as this example from the 1860s attributed to Zuber & Cie of Rixheim, were recommended for billiard rooms or restaurants.

*Right* A fragment of the frieze portion of 'Décor Jardin d'Hiver', designed by Edouard Muller in 1853 and block-printed by Jules Defossé, who was in partnership with Hippolyte Karth from 1863, after which this design continued to be produced. It is the only evidence to date of Sanderson's dealings with one of the most important Parisian wallpaper manufacturers of the mid-nineteenth century.

*Right* A Balin imitation of eighteenth-century whitework, composed of embossed paper and muslin.

*Opposite* Balin's ability to imitate even the most subtle of textiles is epitomised by this example, inspired by a seventeenth-century Persian silk satin with metal thread embroidery.

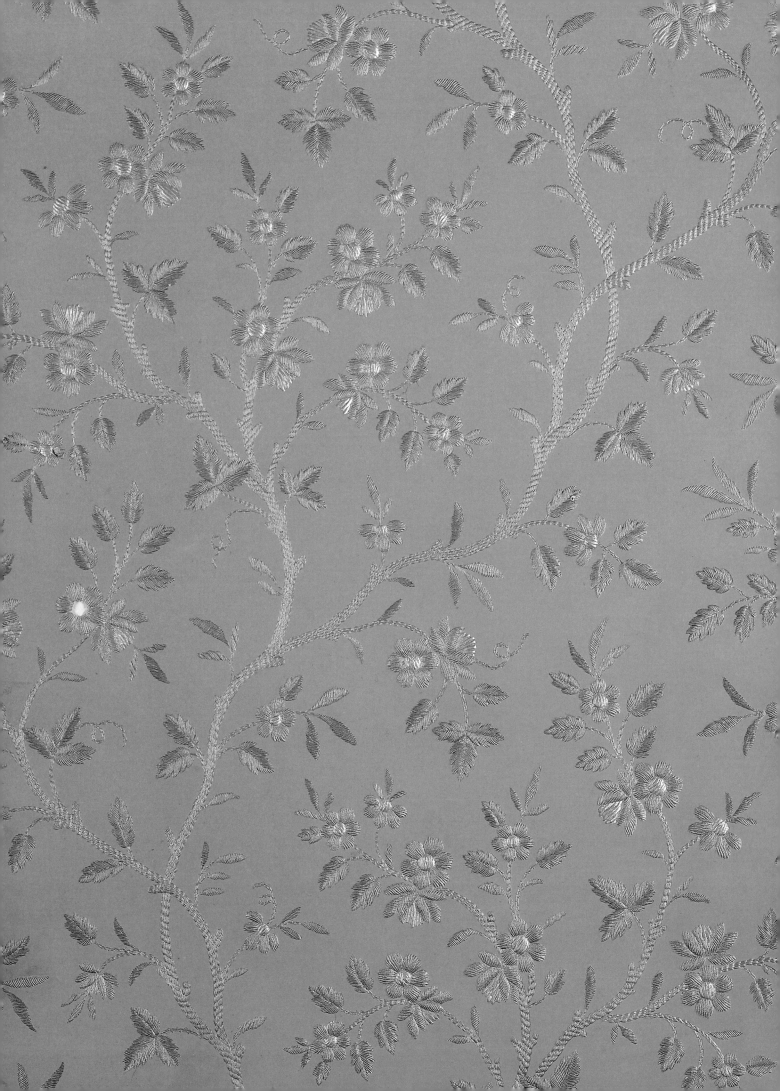

*Above* Balin's expensive imitation leathers were made from block-printed paper that was painted, gilded, embossed and varnished. Balin took this design, stamped 'Louis XVI', from an eighteenth-century Italian leather in his personal collection.

*Above left* Inspired by an Italian Renaissance
velvet then in a private collection, Balin's pattern
No. 5190, dating from the late 1860s, replicates
appliqué and couched gold cord.

*Above right* This Balin paper of about 1870
reproduces a sixteenth-century silk from his
personal collection. It is block-printed, gilded
and embossed to replicate laid- and couched-
work embroidery.

Exhibition and all the major decorative arts collections began to acquire his embossed wallpapers, ensuring the exposure of his products to a wider audience. Sanderson, meanwhile, had the sole British agency for Balin wallpapers.

We may never know what propelled Sanderson to take up his new role as an importer of French wallpapers, but it was a propitious time to do so. The Cobden–Chevalier Treaty of 1860 ushered in a period during which punitive duties on some 1,400 classes of manufactured French goods, including papers, were removed or reduced by the British government. During the 1860s and 1870s many among the emerging nouveau riche were building elegant houses and furnishing them with ostentatious goods including the luxurious and expensive papers imported by Sanderson. It was later recorded that his 'intimate knowledge of the trade and industrious business habits soon raised the firm to the position of the first house in the trade'.[7] By 1865 he needed larger premises and on 25 May moved with his wife and family – now comprising three sons and a daughter born that very day –

to 52 Berners Street, where the elegant Georgian houses were still largely residential. Dealing only with the trade, by this time he numbered among his clients the pre-eminent decorators, upholsterers and cabinetmakers Messrs Cowtan & Sons Ltd, which had been founded in the eighteenth century and was based in nearby Oxford Street from the 1830s until the 1930s. Their wallpaper order books from 1824 to 1938 survive and record numerous papers obtained from Sanderson, including one order in 1866 for eighteen pieces of French paper, presumably by Balin, 'gold impressed'.[8]

As the 1860s progressed, however, there were an increasing number of English voices calling for design reform – that is, far less dependence on elaborate Continental designs and products, as well as flatter patterns more appropriate for wallpapers and textiles. Sanderson would have been aware of this trend.[9] As early as 1862, the International Exhibition held in London had prompted criticism of the ornate and realistic French style; most of the prizes went to English firms, who also fared well at the

Paris Exposition Universelle in 1867, being praised for their 'sober, conventional treatments of foliage, exhibiting considerable skill in design and arrangement'.[10] Metford Warner, a junior partner at the highly regarded wallpaper manufacturer Jeffrey & Co. in 1866, declared soon afterwards that despite 'some of the most beautiful paperhangings ever produced being those printed and embossed by M. Balin, still they after all bring no credit to the designer of this day.'[11] Even more influential was Charles L. Eastlake's view, first expressed in his 1868 *Hints on Household Taste*, that patterns should be conventionalised, even austere, as he promoted wallpapers in ready-made sets for use below the dado rail, as fillings above it and with a frieze at the top.[12]

Arthur Sanderson must have begun having papers manufactured to his 'private' designs at about this point, since his trademark (no. 178,867) was noted as having been 'used by applicants and predecessors in business since upwards of six years before the 13th August 1875.'[13] His early wallpaper designs appear not to have been made in France, but by English manu-

facturers, including Carlisle & Clegg, which suggests some earlier connection between Sanderson and this Islington firm. Surviving examples show a transition from ornamental three-dimensional renderings to conventionalised floral patterns of the sort promoted by leading design reformers such as Owen Jones, William Morris and Eastlake.

By 1872 Sanderson's success necessitated the removal of his family to Kensington so that the Berners Street premises could be devoted to his growing business. During this decade the demand for papers increased, as mechanisation – begun in earnest in Britain in the 1840s – stimulated a dramatic surge in wallpaper production, which rose from 5.5 million rolls annually in 1851 to 32 million in 1874.[14] As manufacturing costs fell in tandem with this increase, a wider choice of fashionable papers became available at reasonable prices. Wallpaper was now an essential element of both grand and modest interiors, as interior decoration itself became a subject of growing interest to authors and journalists. Although Sanderson continued to import papers, his attention increasingly turned to his own commission-printed designs. These were block-printed by hand and thus some seven times more costly than machine-made papers, but they were still less expensive than his French papers. The rapidly increasing wealth of the British urban middle classes provided a ready market for his moderately priced and locally made wares, encouraging Sanderson to expand his range of commission-printed wallpapers further to satisfy varied tastes and purses. To assist in this expansion, in 1877 his oldest son, John, completed his training in wallpaper manufacture and entered the firm at the age of eighteen.

Arthur Sanderson had made his name as one of England's largest dealers in foreign goods and the firm remained sole agents for Balin papers as late as 1901. However, by then he was already best remembered for manufacturing his own products. As an article in *Commerce* recalled: 'the rise of a new school in England, the growth of a demand for British goods, and a feeling that he could manufacture first-hand a better article than was then being put on the market,' encouraged Arthur Sanderson to purchase land in Chiswick for a wallpaper factory, where in 1879 he began block-printing his own designs for the firm's exclusive use.[15] In just under twenty years, Sanderson's place in the world of wallpaper manufacture had been established.

*Opposite, left* The design in this Balin leather paper of the 1870s is identical to that shown on page 16, but with the addition of an embossed Japaneseque background.

*Opposite, right* The Sanderson trademark was in use by at least 1869; its rose, shamrock and thistle motifs represent England, Ireland and Scotland.

*Right* Block-printed (wet on dry) in England for Arthur Sanderson, these 'Chrysanthemum' papers illustrate the dado (*bottom*), filling (*centre*) and frieze (*top*) arrangement that became fashionable in the 1870s. The filling is in a style similar to William Morris's 'Marigold' of 1875.

*Overleaf* Dado, filling and frieze arrangement illustrated in a painted and stencilled dining room of 1890, designed by Joseph Sharp of Glasgow.

# Of Exceptional Quality and Taste

¶ By 1881 three of Arthur Sanderson's sons – John, Arthur Bengough and Harold – are involved in the business, now trading as Arthur Sanderson & Sons.

¶ Arthur dies in March 1882; as late as 1890 he is 'still held in affectionate esteem by the whole of the decorating trade, many of whose members owe much to his assistance and advice'.

¶ Arthur Bengough Sanderson introduces flat screens for displaying wallpaper at the company's showroom in Berners Street.

¶ In 1884 the Sanderson brothers acquire the merchanting and importing business of A. J. Duff.

¶ The firm wins a gold medal at the New Orleans World Exposition in 1885.

¶ Ingrain papers are introduced in 1885.

¶ In 1886 Japanese papers begin to be imported; within a few years papers are also being imported from Germany.

¶ The 1880s building boom in Britain greatly increases the demand for affordable wallpapers.

¶ Surface-printing machines are added at the Chiswick factory by at least 1885; the first standbook of machine-printed patterns is issued in 1887.

¶ By 1890 the three brothers have doubled the volume of the company's trade since 1882.

¶ A four-storey factory is built at Chiswick in 1892–93 to accompany the single-storey building built shortly after Arthur Sanderson's death.

¶ Harold oversees production and design; his freelance designers include A. F. Brophy, Christopher Dresser, George Haité, the Silver Studio and C. F. A. Voysey.

The little factory that Arthur Sanderson built in 1879 in Chiswick, just under 9 miles west of his Berners Street showroom, was hardly bigger than a domestic building, but it was large enough to house the ten block-printers who initially produced patterns of 'simple character' to complement the elaborate papers that Sanderson continued to import from several French firms. His firm was in the vanguard of the eighty-odd British companies in the late 1870s that combined wallpaper manufacture with merchanting of products made elsewhere.[1] Sanderson's good relationship with Bezault & Pattey *fils* made it possible for his oldest son, John (1859–1915), to train in its Paris works for six months in 1877. Entering the family business immediately upon his return, John Sanderson took charge of sales, travelling throughout Britain to take orders from trade and retail decorators, anticipating their diverse needs and keeping an eye on regional trends; this proved so successful an approach that by 1885 the firm employed four 'travellers'. Arthur Bengough Sanderson, the second son (1861–1946), joined the firm in 1881, taking charge of the accounts at Berners Street. By then the third son, Harold (1863–1958), was already one year into his apprenticeship as a block-printer at the Chiswick factory. Harold's supervising printer was a Frenchman, a fact that further confirms the close and cordial contacts Arthur Sanderson had developed with Parisian wallpaper manufacturers. Arthur's sights, however, were firmly set on the creation of a uniquely English wallpaper company.

Arthur Sanderson died in the spring of 1882, as he approached his fifty-third birthday.[2] He left behind not only his second wife, Louisa, and eleven children, including three sons now fully involved in the business, but also what was clearly a sizeable amount of good will. Even as late as 1890, the *Journal of Decorative Art* would recall that he 'left a name which is still held in affectionate esteem by the whole of the decorating trade, many of whose members owe much to his assistance and advice'.[3]

Personalised advice was one of the firm's hallmarks; in the same article a Sanderson staff member described the considerable amount of time spent at Berners Street trying to locate old or unidentified patterns for clients. 'Every day brings us a batch of inquiries, but our customers appreciate the trouble we take in these matters; many valued accounts and permanent business relations have originated in our finding for a decorator a pattern, which, unaided, he could never have discovered.'[4] The firm's advisory service was bolstered by its wide selection of available patterns and its ability to fill bespoke orders very quickly. Arthur Bengough Sanderson had already seen the advantage of having the firm's entire range shown on screens in the showroom. Since the Sanderson brothers lived in the family home next to the Chiswick works, the company was able to take an order one day and personally instruct the factory the next morning. With the installation of telephones in 1887, communication became even more rapid.

Under the three brothers the range became more diverse. In two books updated regularly, a practice said to be unique to the Sandersons, they displayed French imported papers, a selection of 'embosses, Venetian patterns for drawing rooms and dining rooms, "splendid" tapestry decorations and designs which resembled silk damask'.[5] By the end of the 1880s papers were also being imported from Germany, although their precise nature is unknown.

From 1886 papers were brought directly from Japan. The craze for all things Japanese had begun among a handful of English collectors two decades before, although it was not until the 1870s that this trend captured the imagination of members of the artistic and fashionable sets. Then, in the 1880s, 'what had been a movement became a mania'.[6] There were two distinctly different expressions of this Japanesque trend in wallpapers.

*Previous page* This 1888 Anglo-Japanese ceiling paper is a 'single print', or single-coloured surface machine-production on a coloured ground.

*Above* Through their acquisition of A. J. Duff in 1884, the Sanderson brothers obtained blocks for Japanese-style wallpapers such as these, first printed in 1874–79 by Corbière & Sons.

*Opposite* 'Magnolia', a Sanderson hand block-printed paper of *c.* 1885, was produced in at least thirteen different colourways.

*Above* This Japanese leather paper border in Cordovan style was imported by the Sanderson brothers in the late 1880s. It sold for 1*s*.6*d*. per yard.

*Left* Detail of a lacquered Japanese leather paper composed of handmade paper with a stencilled ground, the embossing foiled and stained.

*Opposite* By the 1890s the Sanderson range of Japanese leather papers often included designs such as this one, which reflects an awareness of developments in Western taste.

*Overleaf* Two Anglo-Japanese designs of *c*. 1888. Block-printed at Chiswick, these sold for 9*s*. per piece, which in 1856 had been standardised in Britain to 12 yards (11 metres). These papers were designed for use on stairways; the decorator could cut them in half lengthwise, forming panels that could be moved up with each stair rise.

The papers initially imported from Japan were similar in appearance to the French offerings that carried bold ornamentation worked in high relief. These Japanese papers also imitated leathers – so much so that they were often called Japanese leather papers – but differed from Continental versions by being much wider and often displaying an overtly Japanese style. Their slightly more pronounced embossing was enhanced by washing a sized ground with gold and stencilling it with additional colours, all sealed with a finish of several layers of lacquer. The Japanese papers' washable surfaces provided a costly, richly coloured alternative to the more subdued English 'sanitaries', which were printed by copper-roller machines in 'oil colours' made from turpentine and resin and available from 1884 in polychrome patterns, often complex Anglo-Japanese designs.[7] Aware of the substantial market for these less costly washable papers, Sanderson offered its own versions in simpler 'aesthetic' or Japanese-inspired patterns, garnering praise for 'the discriminating taste which has guided [their] selection and arrangement'.[8] In addition to these inexpensive washable papers, the Sanderson brothers also produced surface-printed papers for the middle-class market featuring typical Anglo-Japanese motifs: ornamental discs or other decorative bosses, fruit blossoms, birds, bamboo and willowy water reeds.

A selection from Sanderson's wide array of patterns won the firm a gold medal at the New Orleans World Exposition, which was held from December 1884 until April 1885. The exact nature of the Sanderson display is unknown, since the brothers never advertised their awards, relying instead on their reputation, by now well established, for high-quality goods. However, the medal suggests that the firm was beginning to take an active interest in the American market, one that most certainly bore fruit within a decade or two.

The firm also sold plain flocks and, from 1885, ingrains, the latter made using a process patented in 1877 by James S. Munroe of Lexington, Massachusetts. In ingrain papers colour is not applied to the surface but instead comes from the cotton and woollen rags that are dyed before being rendered into pulp. ('Ingrain' in this context should not be confused with woodchip paper – sometimes also called ingrain – which has two layers of paper with wood fibre placed in between, a method perfected in Germany in 1864.) Such papers suited the increasing desire for subtle 'aesthetic' textures and soft or jewel-like tones; they were also heavy and could mask plastered walls that were less than perfect in finish. Ingrains in particular were a shrewd addition to the Sanderson range. They could be printed as well as left plain, and provided a rich 'broken' surface that, in the words of a company historian fifty years later, 'led to large developments in the wallpaper trade'.[9]

Alongside their expanding range of wallpapers, the Sanderson brothers carried other types of products, demonstrating the

inclination for diversification that would remain characteristic of the firm. They stocked papers originally developed for use in ammunition, including cartridge paper (so-called because it was used to form the tube section of a shotgun shell), which they promoted as 'invaluable for large working drawings'.[10] They also sold pounces – papers for stencilling and for transferring embroidery designs from paper to cloth. A singular innovation during the 1880s was the introduction of 'new and cheap picture-rod mouldings…to use below friezes'.[11] These were carried in many styles and sizes, so many that, together with reserve stocks of the firm's Chiswick production, they had to be stored in another building a minute's walk away in Wells Street.

The wallpaper printing itself was now done in a single-storey factory, which had been built shortly after Arthur Sanderson's death. This at first housed some dozen block-printers, but when the increase in business prompted the addition of surface-printing machines, the hand-printing was moved, together with the paper store, to a four-storey building constructed in 1892–93. In the eight years up to 1890 the three brothers had doubled the volume of their company's trade, increasing their printing machines from one to two, and then to eight, all under the watchful eye of Harold Sanderson, who was to remain in charge of the works until 1934.

The Sanderson brothers issued their first standbook of machine-printed patterns in 1887; two more followed in 1888. The 1888 single-print designs were praised for their simplicity

and avoidance of florid multi-colour decoration (which was then drawing criticism as a great flaw in machine-prints) and described as 'of exceptional quality and taste'. The firm's cheaper book of 'oaks, marbles, tiles, and sanitaries, varnished and unvarnished' was noted as a 'useful and varied selection… that should find a ready and large sale'.[12] These inexpensive designs retailed for about 1s. per piece, compared to £2 to £5 for the most expensive wall fillings from Yokohama sold by the firm, indicating the breadth of clientele it now catered for.[13]

The firm also grew as a result of its 1884 acquisition of the merchanting and importing business of A. J. Duff of Bread Street, London. A. J. Duff was himself the successor to Corbière Son & Brindle, also known as Corbière & Sons, established in about 1854 with ironmongery, lamp and fancy furniture departments as well as a paperhanging department. In 1880 the paperhanging department came under the charge of Duff, an employee of over fourteen years.[14] Like Sanderson, Corbière was originally an importing house, although it sold not only French goods, but also patterns. By the time it was transferred into Duff's hands the firm was much changed, being known as 'an exporting house, sending to France patterns and designs for goods which it obtains from South Kensington'.[15]

'South Kensington' in this context meant what is today the Royal College of Art, informally known then as the South Kensington Schools.[16] Corbière had as early as the mid-1860s

*Opposite* This 1890 drawing made in the Chiswick factory illustrates block-printing on the left and, on the right, the system of finishing printed lengths, which were hung up and dried using a gentle heat from steam pipes and fans. According to the *Journal of Decorative Art*, in which this plate appeared, this method, as opposed to the more typical process of racing the paper over hot pans, preserved the delicacy and durability of the colours.

*Above* Detail of a photograph probably taken on the occasion of the firm's fiftieth anniversary in 1910, showing, from left, Harold, John and Arthur Bengough Sanderson.

*Right* These four examples from the 1880s demonstrate how the decorator could combine various papers to create an Anglo-Japanese ensemble. Such papers were inexpensive: the filling and dado paper sold for 3*d.* and 4*d.* per piece, respectively, and the frieze for 4½*d.* per yard. Their low cost was the result of machine-printing, that is, by surface-roller machine.

*Right* 'Pergolese', a single-print paper, was issued in several colourways in 1887, when the Sanderson brothers released their first standbook of papers produced on a surface-roller machine. The filling sold for 4*d.*, but could also be obtained with the addition of tiny block-printed gold dots for 7*d.*

*Below left* Like the other papers illustrated on this page, the rich but limited tones of this Anglo-Japanese stair paper reflect the 1880s trend towards subdued, harmonious colours.

*Below right* Hand block-printed in 1888, this filling and dado paper suggest a hand-woven velvet. At 12*d.* per yard, the dado paper cost four times that of the machine-printed 'Pergolese' border shown above it.

*Above left* Among the most elaborate of papers block-printed at Chiswick were the dado and frieze papers shown here, which were issued *c.* 1887. Broken and unbroken lines printed in gold create an illusion of depth in the frieze.

*Above right* This block-printed mosaic-style paper of the late 1880s was produced in both practical varnished and cheaper unvarnished versions.

acquired designs from at least two students at the Royal College: Maria Brooks and a Kingman, probably George Kingman.[17] The Sanderson brothers may have obtained designs from similar sources, even prior to their acquisition of Corbière's stock and patterns. Certainly the Sanderson firm was later very supportive of young designers and their tutors, and used patterns by A. F. Brophy, who was an art master at the Royal College from at least 1881 until 1883. In 1883 Brophy became headmaster of the Finsbury Technical College, then the training institute for the London City & Guilds designers' qualifications, and it is possible that Sanderson acquired patterns from this channel as well.

Brophy had established his own practice in 1877, which supplied designs for fabrics, furniture, glass, metal and wallpaper. Brophy's patterns were bought by most of the major wallpaper manufacturers, among them Jeffrey & Co., Charles Knowles, Wm Woollams & Co. and Zuber & Cie, so his output was by no means exclusive to the Sandersons. However, it did bring notice, as when one Brophy design for the firm was described as 'simply magnificent'. The same report, in the April 1887 issue of the *Journal of Decorative Art*, notes Brophy's Adams-style 'complete decoration' –

meaning the fashionable ensemble of dado, filling and frieze – as 'of quiet classic dignity and value', although Brophy also produced patterns to suit the Japanesque tastes that had characterised the most fashionable interiors for the past ten years. The article records that the same Sanderson collection contained designs by C. F. A. Voysey and 'other equally good men'.[18] Voysey, who was to become one of the best-known designers of this period, also provided patterns for other firms from 1883, including Jeffrey, Knowles, Woollams and Essex & Co. Essex & Co., in particular, was to become known for its several hundred patterns by Voysey, which were produced from 1891.

This was a period of intense competition within the British wallpaper industry. Sanderson and others in the trade were all purchasing designs from prominent designers such as Christopher Dresser, George Haité and the Silver Studio. Yet little is known about the source of specific Sanderson designs from this time, as the company's surviving pattern records do not begin until 1899. One can only gain an insight into Sanderson's trade and house style by considering the milieu in which it operated, which is the subject of the following chapter.

*Opposite and below left* Block-printed in 1876 by Corbière Son & Brindle, these patterns are attributed to Christopher Dresser, who taught at the South Kensington schools from 1855–68. In 1999 the larger pattern (*opposite*) was screen-printed by Sanderson for the restoration of the Glenview Mansion in Yonkers, New York State, at the request of the project architect, Paige Cowley.

*Below right* Corbière's patterns, including this example registered in 1876, were acquired by Sanderson in 1884.

*Overleaf* In the Sanderson archive are several Japanese books of block-printed motifs marked 'C. Dresser'. Dresser visited Japan in 1876 as an official representative of the British government.

○梨へ熱咳をやめ渇をと
め痰を消し大便を
利し小便をつうず

○棗へ中を補ひ脾と和し
益の氣を補ひ脾を和し
氣をふさぐを治しかつ津
をましー心腹の邪氣と
痰とを去ーしー心肺
をましー腸胃紙

○栗へ氣を補ひ腰脚を
わろー腎を補ひ腰脚
ぐひ氣をめ治し芽栗

○柚へ食を消し酒毒を解
腸胃の悪氣をさり婦人
ー孕で食をおすなどを消

梨

棗

栗

柑

柚

3

# The Milieu

¶ Wm Woollams & Co., established by 1807. After its closure in 1901 its designs and blocks are acquired by Sanderson.

¶ Charles Knowles & Co., founded 1852; purchased by Sanderson at the end of 1913. The commercial side of the business is then moved to Berners Street.

¶ Jeffrey & Co., founded 1864 from an amalgamation of Jeffrey, Wise & Co. and Holmes & Aubert; purchased by the WPM in 1924. Distribution is transferred to 53 Berners Street by 1926; blocks and machines are moved to Sanderson's Chiswick factory by 1927.

¶ Morris & Co., founded 1861; first wallpaper available in 1864; printing transferred to Sanderson's Chiswick factory in 1927. The wallpaper side of the business – including patterns, blocks and company trademark – is acquired by Sanderson in 1940.

¶ John Line, founded *c*. 1880; joined the WPM in 1899. Its patterns are acquired by the Sanderson archive via the WPM in 1962.

¶ Essex & Co., founded 1887; its showroom is purchased by Sanderson in 1923.

¶ Shand Kydd, founded 1891. As a Crown (WPM) brand, its wallcoverings are merchanted by Sanderson from 1973 until the early 1980s.

¶ Percy Heffer, founded 1893; known as Heffer, Scott & Co. from 1912. Sanderson purchases a controlling interest in 1928.

I n the two decades either side of 1900 there were so many wall-paper manufacturers, agents and designers in Britain that its influence was felt on the Continent and as far afield as North America, Australia and New Zealand. Thirty-one British factories – among them those belonging to Sanderson, Carlisle & Clegg[1] and Essex & Co. – came together in 1899 with the formation of the Wallpaper Manufacturers' Association (WPM), but several prominent firms remained independent for a time. These included Percy Heffer, John Line, Jeffrey (printing for Morris & Co.), Knowles, Shand Kydd and Woollams. All ultimately had their patterns, records or entire businesses absorbed by Sanderson. Although Sanderson's factory joined the WPM, its merchanting business at Berners Street remained independent, a critical determinant for the survival of its reputation and name. In outlasting and absorbing many of its competitors, Sanderson gained an archive that today contains one of the finest selections of designs from this period, rivalled only by the holdings of a handful of museums worldwide. Below are brief descriptions of the companies, in order of their formation.

## Wm Woollams & Co.

William Woollams (1782–1840) began his career as an apprentice to John Sherringham, a master paper-stainer. By 1837 Woollams had a factory near Manchester Square in London, where he printed papers for J. G. Crace and other clients. Two of

his three sons, William (*d.* 1859) and Henry (*d.* 1876), carried on the business, which in 1876 passed to their cousin Frederic Aumonier, who had been Henry's assistant since 1853. Innovations credited to Woollams were the introduction of stamped gold papers in 1864, embossed leather papers in 1866 and surface-modelled raised flocks, a technique invented by Aumonier in 1878. In 1848, when 'very few firms aimed at excellence,' Woollams won its first medal, for 'a rich arabesque pilaster printed from 120 blocks'.[2] The firm subsequently received many more awards, including gold medals at the 1884 International Health Exhibition (when Aumonier's efforts to remove arsenic from wallpaper pigments were acknowledged), the 1889 Exposition Universelle and the 1897 Victorian Art Exhibition. By then it had been showing machine-printed papers for two years, and already sold a wide range of papers manufactured by other firms.

Woollams's attempt to broaden its range was unsuccessful. New embossed products such as Lincrusta-Walton (invented by Frederick Walton in 1877 and one-third the price of Balin papers) and Anaglypta (invented by 1886 by Thomas J. Palmer, the manager of Walton's showroom) had brought additional pressure on suppliers that, like Woollams, sold primarily at the top end of the market. Early in 1901 *Commerce* reported the recent closure of Woollams and, together with its designs and blocks, the transfer of one partner, Mr Webbe, to Messers Sanderson. As a result, 'the

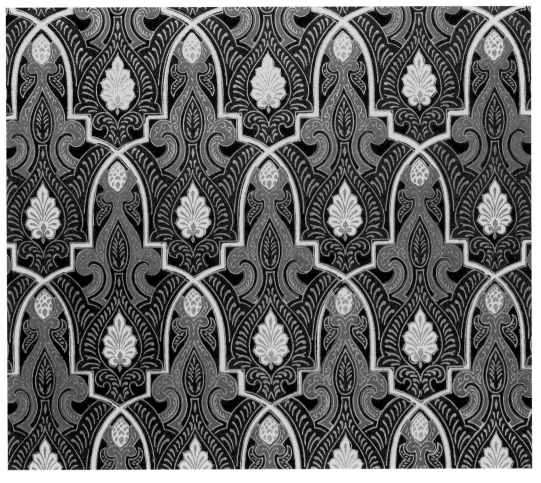

*Previous page* A Charles Knowles paper designed in 1901–2.

*Opposite* Portion of the 'Lion and Dove' frieze by Walter Crane, designed in 1900 to accompany a filling called 'Rose Bush', both block-printed by Jeffrey & Co.

*Left* Block-printed with pigments and gold by Wm Woollams & Co. in 1852, this design by Owen Jones is related to the casts reproduced in vol. 3 (plate XX, no. 32) of his 1841 publication, *La Alhambra*.

*Below left* 'The Brinton', by A. W. N. Pugin, was one of several designs composed for the decorating firm J. G. Crace in 1848 and block-printed by Samuel Scott. It was used in the decoration of the Palace of Westminster, 1851–59, and the blocks later passed to Heffer, Scott & Co.

*Below right* Two colourways of 'Ewan', a flocked paper designed by Owen Jones *c.* 1860 for Jeffrey & Co. Sanderson still retain blocks for this pattern, which were re-cut in 1973.

*Above left* 'Moresque', designed in 1858 by Owen Jones, was block-printed by John Trumble & Sons of Leeds, which joined the WPM in 1899. Trumble's papers eventually came to the Sanderson archive via the WPM.

*Above right* 'The Garden' was in the Wm Woollams & Co. range prior to 1891, when it appeared in a large stand-book, which showed two widths pasted together, as seen here.

*Right* The 1873 design for 'Lily' by William Morris for Morris & Co., with instructions for colouring attached.

*Opposite* Block-printed with a back pattern that shows the influence of the design theories of William Morris, this paper was produced by Knowles in the 1890s.

*Right* Two pages from the
logbooks of Jeffrey & Co.
On the right is a page of
'Dr Dresser's Patterns' block-
printed in 1879; on the left are
examples of the first 'Machine
Golds', produced in 1883.

*Opposite, left* A detail of 'La
Margarete' by Walter Crane,
part of the first set of papers
designed by Crane for Jeffrey
& Co., for the Philadelphia
Centennial Exhibition in 1876.

*Opposite, right* A Jeffrey & Co.
logbook showing, at the
bottom, a portion of 'Sunflower
Frieze' by B. J. Talbert;
introduced in 1879, the frieze
was illustrated in *Ornamental
Interiors* in 1887.

wonderful designs of past masters of the art, such as Owen Jones, will shortly appear in new colourings'.[3]

Woollams produced patterns by Louisa Aumonier, A. F. Brophy, Owen W. Davis, Charles L. Eastlake, George Haité, J. A. Heaton, Owen Jones, G. T. Robinson, Arthur Silver and C. F. A. Voysey, among others. Designs by T. W. Hay and F. J. Weidemann were produced by Woollams and/or Jeffrey & Co.[4]

### Charles Knowles & Co.

Based on the King's Road, Chelsea, Charles Knowles was largely known for its block-printed papers. By 1886 George Haité was one of its chief designers, and in 1892 the firm began to produce machine-printed papers, becoming famous for its chintz, damask and striped designs. Known briefly as Knowles & Essex (1882–86, see Essex & Co.), the firm became a limited company in 1898, later opening a showroom in the West End. Early in the twentieth century its products were praised for their fresh and wholesome colour and patterns: 'The Knowles paper is never muddy; it sparkles, it *smiles* at you; it suggests brightness, joyousness, the optimistic as opposed to the pessimistic side of things.'[5] At the Franco-British Exhibition in 1908, where the firm was awarded a gold medal for its excellent reproduction of older styles, Knowles showed a wide range of papers, including a number of hand- and machine-printed crown decorations, which incorporated a pattern at the top of an otherwise simple design, dispensing with the need for a separate frieze and filling. Among their crown patterns of 1912 was one with a garland of sweet peas on a grey-and-white striped ground, which sold for 5*s*.6*d*. per 11-foot length (about £20 per 3.35 metres today). Arthur Sanderson & Sons purchased Knowles at the end of 1913, transferring the commercial side of the business to Berners Street. Among the records still in the Sanderson archive is a logbook of *c*. 1840–1912 and another from 1907–14.

The firm is known to have produced patterns by A. F. Brophy, Christopher Dresser, George Haité, Sidney Hayward, Arthur Silver, C. F. A. Voysey and Arthur Wilcock.

### Jeffrey & Co.

Jeffrey & Co. formed in 1864 from an amalgamation of Jeffrey, Wise & Co. and its successors (founded *c*. 1836 in Whitechapel), and Holmes & Aubert (active in Islington prior to 1860).[6] Jeffrey & Co. gradually came to public notice when it began printing papers for Morris & Co. in 1864, and more immediately in 1865, when Jackson & Graham gave the firm the order for a large group of patterns by Owen Jones, intended for the Viceroy's Palace in Cairo. *Wyman's Commercial Encyclopaedia* of 1888 notes that the firm since then had 'taken advantage of securing the best British talent. In this way they have done much to raise the tone of English wall-papers, and to stop the old belief that if a design had merit it must necessarily have come from abroad. It is

for this reason that their annual collection of new designs is always rich in novelties, which are there not merely for novelty's sake, but because they have merit in design and are in harmony with the prevailing taste of the day.'

This progress is credited to Metford Warner (1843–1930), who joined the firm in 1866 as a junior partner and was sole proprietor by 1871. In 1872 he introduced frieze, filling and dado schemes devised for him by the Ipswich architect Brightwen Binyon, possibly as a result of Jeffrey & Co.'s association with Charles L. Eastlake. Warner, both an idealist and successful businessman, became known for his sympathetic treatment of designs and for his emphasis on publicly acknowledging designers' names. He won admission for wallpapers in the 1873 Fine Arts Exhibition held at the Royal Albert Hall in London, an event considered the turning point in their regard as a serious artistic medium. Numerous other victories followed, including a gold medal at the 1878 Exposition Universelle, and other medals in Paris (1889 and 1900), Philadelphia (1876), Melbourne (1880), Adelaide (1887) and Chicago (1893). Jeffrey & Co.'s papers also received numerous awards in Britain, the first of which was at the 1862 International Exhibition in London. In 1898 Warner's sons Horace and Albert were taken into partnership and Jeffrey patterns continued to be cited for their artistic merit.

In 1923 the firm was incorporated, but with the retirement of Metford Warner in 1924, it was acquired by the WPM and

Horace and Albert Warner became designers at Sanderson's Chiswick works. Within two years distribution had been transferred to 53 Berners Street – where the 'Jeffrey Gallery' honoured the long-standing reputation of the firm – while the blocks and machines were moved to Sanderson's Chiswick factory by 1927. Among the surviving records is a pattern book of *c.* 1852–74.

Jeffrey & Co. is known to have produced patterns by G. A. Audsley, H. W. Batley, B. Binyon, A. F. Brophy, William Burges, Lindsay Butterfield, Walter Crane, Owen W. Davis, Lewis F. Day, Christopher Dresser, Charles L. Eastlake, Kate Faulkner, G. E. Fox, E. W. Godwin, James Huntington, Owen Jones, A. H. Macmurdo for the Century Guild, Albert Moore, W. Scott Morton, W. J. Muckley, W. J. Neatby, J. D. Sedding, T. W. Sharp, Heywood Sumner, Bruce Talbert, Allan Vigers, C. F. A. Voysey, George Walton, Albert and Horace Warner and Henry Wilson.

## Morris & Co.

The first attempts to print wallpaper at Morris, Marshall, Faulkner & Co. (Morris & Co. from 1875) were carried out in 1861–62 by William Morris (1834–1896) using transparent colours and zinc plates. When these were unsuccessful, he turned the printing over to Jeffrey & Co., who used the traditional method of block-printing with opaque pigments, although transparent tones were later achieved. Between 1864 and 1874 only ten patterns were issued, half of which were adaptations of older patterns. Thereafter Morris's designs often incorporated the bold arrangement of a coiling or meandering stem for which he is now admired; indeed, despite the many designs he created for books, furniture, stained glass, tapestries and textiles, he is perhaps best known today for his wallpapers. In total Morris designed over fifty wallpapers, including five ceiling papers, and another forty-nine patterns were supplied by other designers.[7] Among these were three ('Carnation', 'Loop Trail' and 'Mallow') designed between 1877 and 1880 by Kate Faulkner, sister to Charles Faulkner, one of the company's original founders.

Although the firm had a small range compared to other wallpaper manufacturers, during the late 1880s Morris & Co.

experimented with additions of flock and mica; it also issued a few machine-prints. Upon Morris's death W. A. S. Benson became chairman; in 1908 he himself designed at least one new pattern, 'Garden Craft', and another, 'Sweet Pea', with John Henry Dearle. Dearle, who had apprenticed with the firm in 1878, became its chief designer in 1890 and its art director in 1896, and was still with the company in 1924–27 when Jeffrey & Co. was absorbed by the WPM and its printing for Morris & Co. was transferred to Sanderson's Chiswick works. Dearle's son Duncan also worked for Morris & Co. and was a director when the firm went into voluntary liquidation in 1940, at which time Sanderson bought the wallpaper side of the business, obtaining the blocks, logbooks and existing stock, as well as the title to the Morris & Co. trademark.

Morris & Co. produced patterns by William Morris and other designers including W. A. S. Benson, J. H. Dearle (whose most notable designs were 'Blackthorn' in 1892 and 'Compton' in 1896), Kate Faulkner, May Morris and George Gilbert Scott the younger (credited with 'Indian').

## John Line

John Line was originally a cabinetmaker in Bath and in 1874 acquired a furniture business in Reading that was subsequently run by his three sons. By 1880 the company had a London agent, L. H. Dayes, and began trading from Reading as a wallpaper wholesaler, offering its first pattern book of 206 papers produced by other manufacturers, printed both by hand and by machine. The designs showed the influence of Pugin and Owen Jones; a few were original blocked and stencilled patterns, many of which were designed for the firm by F. G. Froggatt. In 1892 the company moved to London and began purchasing designs from the leading studios. These designs proved so successful that the company built a block-printing factory at Southall in 1906 to produce them. By the same year complete decorative schemes could be printed to customers' specifications and the firm also had premises in Manchester. Two years later John Line received a gold medal for wallpapers at the Franco-British Exhibition.

By the 1920s John Line was known for its exclusive, innovative products, such as the first wallpaper decoration featuring a large cut-out 'growth' (not to be confused with 'drop-down' borders with cut-out edges, which Sanderson was offering prior to the First World War). From this point until 1940 the firm was instrumental in the revival of scenic papers featuring modernist motifs, and also produced romanticised landscapes. The company remained well known in the 1950s for its flock wallpapers, as well as for its range of modern designs. Its patterns were acquired by the Sanderson archive as a result of a complex series of share purchases involving KL Holdings in 1958, and the subsequent sale of a majority of these to the WPM in 1962.

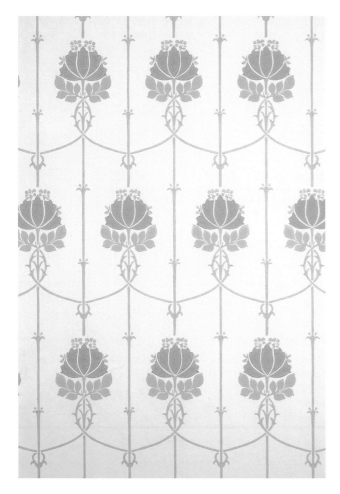

John Line produced patterns during this period by Christopher Dresser, F. G. Froggatt, the Silver Studio, C. F. A. Voysey, William J. Neatby (who was head designer from 1907 to 1910) and William W. C. Pitts (who worked in the design studio *c.* 1907 and was head designer from *c.* 1921 to 1936).

## Essex & Co.

Essex & Co. was founded in 1887 by R. Walter Essex, who had previously worked for a number of other wallpaper factories and had been a partner at Knowles & Essex from 1882 until 1886 (see Charles Knowles & Co.). Essex began as a wallpaper merchant and did not manufacture his own papers until 1891, when a factory was built on Lavender Hill, Battersea, for printing by both block and machine. Its speciality was hand-printed and stencilled friezes, produced in a department that was managed at first by F. Graham Rice and later by John Illingworth Kay, who had worked in the Silver Studio from *c.* 1892 until 1900, when he joined Essex & Co., remaining there until 1922. Known as an original and enterprising manufacturer, Essex & Co. produced papers by many well-known designers, but was especially associated with C. F. A. Voysey because it printed the majority of his designs after 1893. When Essex & Co. joined the WPM in 1899 it continued to promote its name independently, and was one of only two English wallpaper manufacturers represented at the 1900 Exposition Universelle in Paris. Two years later the *Journal of Decorative Art* declared that 'an "Essex" wallpaper has been the synonym for a specific quality of excellence – the hallmark of artistic thought and artistic expression in decorative art', adding that 'to speak of an "Essex" paper is to speak of what is superlatively original and good, even in an age when originality is almost a common denominator'.[8] When the firm's showroom was bought by Sanderson in 1923, the Essex name was retained for a number of years while many of the early Voysey designs were successfully revived.

Essex & Co. patterns were designed by Albert J. Baker, Lindsay Butterfield, George Haité, John Illingworth Kay, Thomas R. Spence, Charles H. Townsend, C. F. A. Voysey and Harrison W. Weir, among others.

*Opposite* Louisa Aumonier, the daughter of Wm Woollams's director, Frederic, probably designed this Woollams wallpaper after *Chrysanthemum*, a painting she exhibited at the Royal Academy in 1885. She worked for the Silver Studio in the 1890s.

*Left and above left* Two early twentieth-century John Line wallpapers, one with a companion border (*left*). Arthur Silver designed Line's trade card in 1891 and his studio thereafter supplied Line with many designs; the stenciled frieze (*above left*) is attributed to Rex Silver, *c.* 1905.

*Opposite* 'Squire's Garden', designed by C. F. A. Voysey based on an embroidered bed-quilt worked by Mrs Reynolds Stephens in 1896, was issued by Essex & Co. as a machine-printed wallpaper in 1898 and shown at the 1900 Exposition Universelle in Paris.

*Left* 'Savaric', a block-printed wallpaper designed *c*. 1896 by Voysey for Essex & Co., was used in a bedroom in Victor Horta's Solway House in Brussels. It remains in the Sanderson hand-print range, supplied to order.

*Overleaf:*

*Top left* Showing a typical range of colourways for the period 1897–1904, this Voysey design was machine-printed by Essex & Co.

*Top right* This stencilled frieze is a later variant of Shand Kydd's peacock pattern, designed by W. Dennington in 1900.

*Bottom left* The Charles Knowles logbooks record that its first machine-printed papers appeared in the 1905–6 season; the examples shown here were designed by (from top down) Roberts, Christopher Dresser, Dresser again, C. F. A. Voysey, Knapp and Shiells.

*Bottom right* 'Monkshood' by Alan F. Vigers, machine-printed by Jeffrey & Co., *c*. 1902.

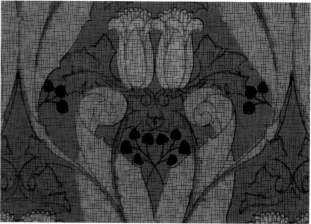

*Above left* Designed by the children's book illustrator Miss Bryant, 'The Trinidad' was first block-printed by Charles Knowles & Co. in 1901–2, and later by Sanderson.

*Above right* This machine-printed John Line wallpaper was intended to imitate a woven textile; it epitomises the English Art Nouveau style of 1900–5.

*Overleaf* Two block-printed Percy Heffer wallpapers of *c.* 1912–15. The design on the left is either by or after C. R. Mackintosh.

## Shand Kydd

William Shand Kydd (1864–1936) worked for several other firms prior to the establishment of his own wallpaper business in Marylebone Road, London, in 1891. Having also trained as a decorative artist at Hayward & Sons (a London firm originating in the seventeenth century that pioneered the re-introduction of stencilled wallpapers in the 1880s), he produced block-printed and stencilled wallpapers. The latter technique added rich colours and surface textures, which were created by using sponges and crumpled chamois skins, as well as a range of different types of brushes, within a blocked outline. At first he cut his own blocks and stencils, but by 1896 he had moved to premises off Tottenham Court Road and was selling papers to taste-making London shops such as Liberty, Maple and Waring, and soon afterwards employed some five block-printers and twelve stencillers. In 1906 a new factory was outfitted in Highgate.

William Shand Kydd was known especially for friezes up until the First World War, and for cut-out decorations in the 1920s; he was ranked with Metford Warner and Harold Sanderson as a major figure in the wallpaper industry.[9] Three decades later, under his son Norman Shand Kydd, the firm he founded still produced fashionable and influential machine-printed papers from its new factory in Christchurch, and continued to do so after 1958, when it merged with John Line. Although not a member of the WPM, it had co-operated with the combine and by 1961 the Shand Kydd factory was a WPM subsidiary operated by KL Holdings. Thereafter, as a Crown (WPM) brand, Shand Kydd wallcoverings continued to be merchanted by Sanderson from 1973 until the early 1980s, when the Christchurch factory closed and many patterns were transferred to the newly consolidated Sanderson archive, then in Uxbridge, with the printing passing to Crown Wallcoverings Ltd.[10] As a result of the sale of Crown Wallcoverings to Borden Decorative Products (USA) in 1985, and subsequent corporate deals between 1999 and 2004, the brand is now issued by Blue Mountain Wallcoverings of Canada.[11]

Many of the patterns created up until the 1920s are thought to have been designed by William Shand Kydd himself. One Mr W. Dennington is known to have designed a 1900 Shand Kydd pattern called 'The Peacock Frieze', which remains in the hall of the Blackwell School, Cumberland.

## Percy Heffer

Trained at Essex & Co., Percy Heffer – known in the trade as 'an irrepressible wag' – was as much a 'modern' as Essex. By 1895 Heffer had a collection noted for its Voysey designs and was soon a regular exhibitor at trade fairs. Two years later his collection was described as 'consistently good alike in colour, design and manufacture'; it also included a frieze by Charles Rennie Mackintosh that was said to represent 'the dissidence of dissent in decorative art' and to display 'a noble unrest against accepted convention and a reaching out to the dim unknown'.[12] In 1912 Heffer took over Scott, Cuthbertson & Co., the wallpaper firm that in 1848 had printed the papers designed by Augustus Welby Pugin for the new Parliament buildings in London. Louis Stahl left Sanderson's studio to become Heffer's chief designer in 1914. By 1915 Heffer had located its showroom next door to Sanderson's at 56 Berners Street. However, Heffer's rejection of bulk production and focus on progressive designs was not financially successful, and Sanderson purchased a controlling interest in the firm in 1928.

Heffer produced or acquired patterns by C. R. Mackintosh, A. W. N. Pugin, Louis Stahl and C. F. A. Voysey, among others.

# *To Serve the Decorator*

¶ 1891: Sanderson has 'marched with the times'.

¶ A new factory building is built at Chiswick in 1893.

¶ Hinged display panels, now standard worldwide, are introduced in the showroom by 1894.

¶ In January 1895 the showroom occupies 53 Berners Street; by April 1901 the company has also leased 51–55; this confirms Sanderson's as the largest wallpaper showroom in London, a boast made as early as 1898.

¶ The Sanderson family home in Chiswick is donated to the town for use as a free library in 1898 when the family moves to Kensington.

¶ In 1899 Sanderson's Chiswick factory joins the Wall Paper Manufacturers Ltd (WPM), a joint-stock combination intended to achieve a monopoly on wallpaper production. The WPM soon controls 98 per cent of the trade.

¶ By this period Sanderson is exporting to the British colonies and the USA.

¶ In 1900 Sanderson acquires the designs and blocks of Wm Woollams & Co., whose designs by Owen Jones are recoloured and offered by Sanderson.

¶ A. Sanderson & Sons becomes a limited company in 1900.

¶ The firm begins selling paints and varnishes in 1900, becoming sole agents for Ripolin, the French paint manufacturer.

¶ A female chemist is appointed at this time: based at Chiswick, Dr Edith Humphrey is thought to be one of the first women to hold such a position in the wallpaper and textile industry.

¶ Between 1902 and 1903 a new factory building designed by C. F. A. Voysey is built at the Chiswick works.

¶ 1902: Sanderson products 'have now become a recognised element in the movement that has placed [Britain] in the premier position in the world for the manufacture of wall-papers'.[1]

By 1890 the Sanderson brothers had established an enviable reputation, being described a year later as a firm that 'have marched with the times, and have kept quite abreast with the public demands in matters of taste'. The same report added: 'This is not a small thing to say, as there have been developments and changes within the last few years sufficient to tax to the utmost the resources of all but the most alert.'[2]

The issue of public taste was of paramount importance. Close to 140,000 new houses were built in London in the ten years up to December 1892, with similar growth in cities such as Birmingham and Glasgow. Most of these new homes were speculative ventures by builders who retained and rented many of their properties. While noting that new laws had made the construction of unsanitary houses unlikely, and that furniture – including carpets – had improved apace, an 1898 article in *The Artist* nonetheless lamented 'No one will deny that nearly every paper put on a house wall "by the landlord" is bad in design and inharmonious in colour,' and 'We have progressed more slowly in our crusade against ugly walls than against any other part of our modern houses.' This, claimed the author, was the reason why 'reform rests largely with the public, and they have but to insist to control the situation.' The public, however, remained dependent on decorators and builders for their selection of wallpapers, and they in turn relied on the trade's pattern books and showrooms. Not surprisingly, Sanderson focused considerable energy on its pattern books and showrooms during this period. Another priority was the continued improvement of the firm's machine-made papers, singled out by *The Artist* as 'demonstrating the fact that good design in wallpapers is not necessarily uncommercial'.[3]

Internal company records suggest that the Berners Street showroom was in a near-constant state of redevelopment and expansion for more than a decade from the early 1890s. By the late 1890s Sanderson claimed to have the largest showroom in London, and the range of products it offered had broadened. Around 1895 the firm became the sole London agent for the products of the Cordelova Company, which, from Pitt Street in Edinburgh, manufactured papier-mâché friezes in imitation of Spanish embossed leather. Ever alert to the needs of the trade, Sanderson began selling paints and varnishes in 1900, at first as sole agents for Ripolin, a paint made in France. Two years later Sanderson introduced a new 'water paint', or washable distemper, called Mayresco.[4] At Berners Street, wallpapers were displayed on hinged screens that swung like doors, devices now

common to wallpaper showrooms worldwide, which were introduced in the Sanderson showroom in the 1890s. Prompt deliveries – a matter of pride at Berners Street – were enhanced by the replacement of horse vans (which had themselves replaced the original fleet of hand trucks) with 'motor vans' between 1900 and 1902. This development coincided with the transformation of the firm into a limited company in 1900, and further expansion of the showroom followed.

Now with the leases to 51–55 Berners Street, John Sanderson, chairman and managing director from 1900, and Arthur Bengough Sanderson, who was in charge of the showroom and merchanting, hired more full-time salesmen to aid the professionals arriving to select papers. These professional decorators were now often accompanied by their clients. However, the firm was at pains not to compete with retail decorators, so much so that it was said to be 'almost as easy to get into the "Marlborough House set" itself as to invade their show-rooms, unless...furnished with an official introduction'. Inside, the setting was described as resembling 'Aladdin's Palace' or 'the late Lord Leighton's wondrous house in Holland Park-road', the latter a reference to the sumptuously decorated residence continually embellished from 1866 until Leighton's death in 1896.[5]

Other changes were made to the Berners Street premises to accommodate office staff, who by 1900 included female typists, the typewriters themselves having been introduced in 1893. The new showrooms of 1901 incorporated a telephone exchange and a system of pneumatic tubes linking all departments. In 1903 electric lights replaced gas. From the dozen employees who worked at Berners Street in 1881, twenty years later the number had increased to over eighty, including the founder's youngest son, Herbert (1881–1971), a chartered accountant who joined the firm in 1903 and worked in this capacity until he enlisted

*Above* A frieze of poppies and chrysanthemums, block-printed *c.* 1895 on a shaded mica ground.

*Previous page* 'The Kelvin', designed by Harry Watkins Wild, was one of the first wallpaper patterns to be surface machine-printed at Sanderson and was produced in many different colourways over several years. No. 31360 is shown here; see page 61 for another.

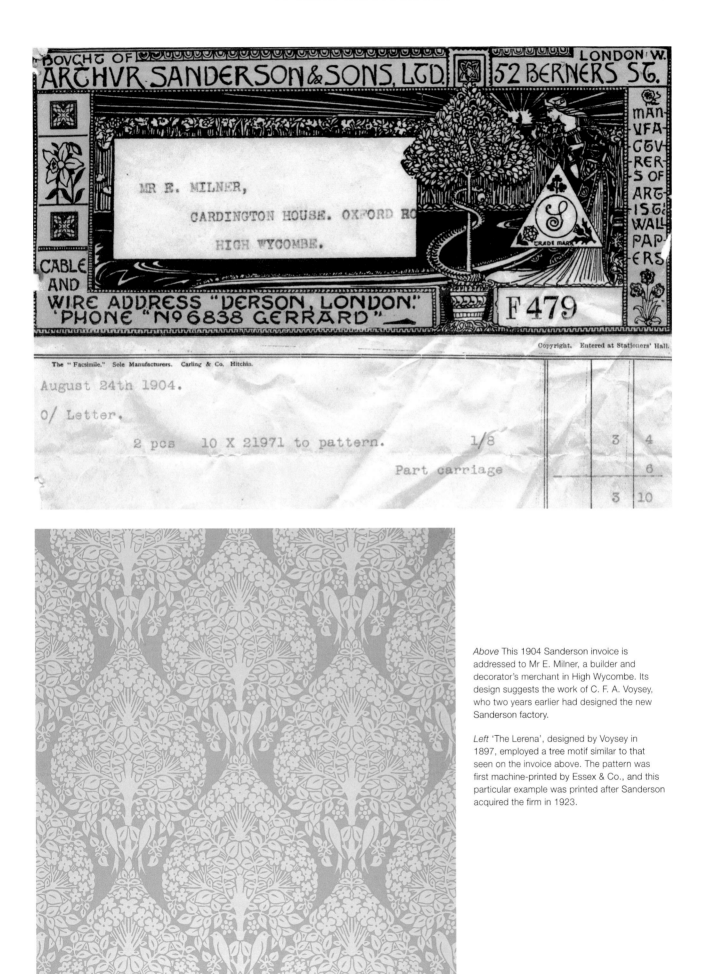

BOVGHT OF ARTHVR SANDERSON & SONS, LTD. 52 BERNERS ST. LONDON W.

MANVFACTVRERS OF ARTISTS WALLPAPERS

MR E. MILNER,

CARDINGTON HOUSE. OXFORD RO

HIGH WYCOMBE.

CABLE AND WIRE ADDRESS "DERSON, LONDON." 'PHONE "Nº 6838 GERRARD"

F 479

Copyright, Entered at Stationers' Hall.

The " Facsimile." Sole Manufacturers. Carling & Co. Hitchin.

August 24th 1904.

O/ Letter.

| | | | | |
|---|---|---|---|---|
| 2 pcs | 10 X 21971 to pattern. | 1/8 | 3 | 4 |
| | Part carriage | | | 6 |
| | | | 3 | 10 |

*Above* This 1904 Sanderson invoice is addressed to Mr E. Milner, a builder and decorator's merchant in High Wycombe. Its design suggests the work of C. F. A. Voysey, who two years earlier had designed the new Sanderson factory.

*Left* 'The Lerena', designed by Voysey in 1897, employed a tree motif similar to that seen on the invoice above. The pattern was first machine-printed by Essex & Co., and this particular example was printed after Sanderson acquired the firm in 1923.

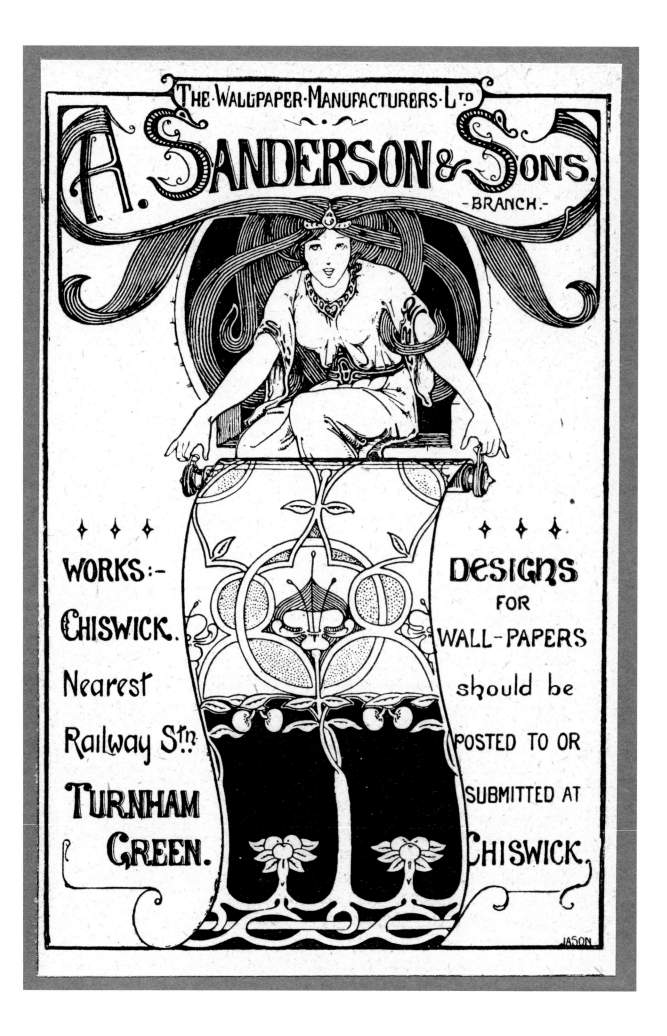

*Opposite* A *c.* 1900 Sanderson advertisement, signed 'Jason', includes a note encouraging designers to submit their work to the Chiswick factory.

*Left* This Adamesque dado panel, block-printed in about 1896, was possibly designed by A. F. Brophy, who had already designed other wallpapers in this style for the Sanderson brothers.

*Below left* 'The Almond Blossom' also dates from *c.* 1896. As a machine-print, selling at 2*s.* per piece (6*d.* per yard for the frieze), it was much less expensive than the Adamesque panel shown above it, which was released in the same year but sold for 5*s.* per piece.

during the First World War. Company minutes document how often the Berners Street premises had to be altered to serve the growing firm's needs, and after various attempts to create better access and working arrangements, substantial rebuilding began in 1906 and was completed the following year.

At the factory equally dramatic changes were taking place. Between 1893 and 1904 many alterations were carried out and two new buildings were erected, the later of the two having been designed by C. F. A. Voysey in 1902.[6] On a site nearly an acre in size, the number of employees rose from 250 in 1896 to 300 just five years later. This was partly due to the transfer of much of the WPM block-printing to Chiswick, with the remainder going to Essex Mills in Battersea. Pattern-book making, once done in Berners Street, was also now part of the Chiswick operation and in 1905 totalled some 12,600 pattern books. Compared to the number of books issued in the previous three years, this figure actually represented a *reduction* in an effort to cut costs, which in 1902 had been as high as £10,000 (some £780,000 today).[7] Among these pattern books were little books, said to have been a Sanderson innovation, intended 'for carrying about when a decorator does not desire to burden himself with a heavy load, or just wishes to get an idea of his client's taste'.[8]

The firm's patterns – especially its machine-prints – were increasingly influencing and changing its customers' tastes. The *Journal of Decorative Art*'s annual commentary on Sanderson

products reveals that by 1891 French and Japanese goods were only a slight part of the business. Soon little was written of sanitaries, and after about 1895 frieze and fillings no longer had dado patterns. In contrast, however, machine-made flocks, mica grounds, damask patterns, 'chintzes', patterned ingrains, staircase decorations, ceiling and bathroom papers – with tile and other 'ceramic' designs – and embosses and finishes of all sorts, including 'satinettes' and moirés, became more important to Sanderson's output and featured prominently in the annual *JDA* articles until about 1905. Both modern and traditional designs were popular during this period. Stripes, both plain and patterned, were in such demand that a book containing 200–300 striped designs was issued in 1904. Block-prints continued to receive notice, while in the early twentieth century increasing praise went to nursery patterns, which were also recommended for use in schools. In its selection of new patterns, Sanderson had an uncanny gift for anticipating future trends: one review of the 1903 'set' exclaimed that Sanderson's 'knowledge of the trade is so intimate, and their sense of its needs so keen, that a glance through their books is like consulting the oracle – the future lies revealed to us'.[9]

The selection, colouring and production of Sanderson designs remained the province of Harold Sanderson, who also exercised wider influence as a WPM board member (where his fellow directors included George Kirby of Carlisle & Clegg).

*Above left* With a surface-printed mica ground and block-printed poppy pattern, this wallpaper is probably the highly successful poppy design created by A. F. Brophy in 1890, after which several other similar designs were issued by Sanderson.

*Above right* This example of 'The Kelvin', by Harry Watkins Wild, *c.* 1896, is surface machine-printed and incorporates a texture suggestive of tapestry. See page 54 for a different colourway.

*Opposite, above* This design for a frieze by Harry Watkins Wild is related to 'The Argosy' of 1902, which was printed with blocked outlines and stencilled infills.

*Opposite, below left* 'The Nana Ceiling', a late nineteenth-century surface-printed paper designed to suggest plasterwork. Its even-coloured ground is wash-printed, that is, with a sieved water-based emulsion.

*Opposite, below right* Detail of 'The Oak Tree', an 1898 surface machine-printed paper by John Illingworth Kay, who was a designer at the Silver Studio from *c.* 1892 to 1900.

As remains the typical practice at Sanderson today, Harold had a small team of designers whose work was augmented by the purchase of patterns from freelance artists. Seventeen designs were purchased from the Silver Studio between early 1893 and early 1898. Others who contributed designs during this period were the Norwegian painter, illustrator and tapestry designer Gerhard Munthe and the Swedish designer Clara Hahr, who contributed four designs to the 1898 collection.[10] From the mid-1890s the well-known English illustrators William S. Coleman and Patten Wilson and the highly regarded designers Arthur Wilcox and George R. Rigby also supplied patterns.[11] Notably, A. F. Brophy provided at least 140 designs between 1900, when company records begin, and his death in 1912. On the staff for a short time was Louis Stahl, a German who joined the firm in the early 1900s, conducted the Sanderson Bleak House Band and produced 'The Cedar Tree', one of the company's best-known designs, before departing in late 1914 to become chief designer at Heffer, Scott & Co.

One long-serving designer who greatly influenced the Sanderson style was Harry Watkins Wild, who joined the studio with the closure of William Cooke & Sons in 1893. Cooke's firm, founded in 1856 and issuing block- and machine-printed papers, was known as 'the most prolific of Dresser's wallpaper collaborations.'[12] Wild was thus familiar with Christopher Dresser's style, which was instrumental in the introduction of authentic

*Opposite* 'The Fulford', number 33386, employs the aesthetic tertiary shades fashionable in the late nineteenth century. Its relatively high price of 2*s*.6*d*. per piece for a single-print machine-produced paper indicates that more costly permanent pigments were used.

*Left* 'The Crocus', a 1905 wallpaper, displays a combination of machine-printing and aerograph-stencilling, the latter a new and labour-intensive technique employing zinc stencils, one for each colour, which were passed from hand to hand along the printing table.

Japanese motifs into Western design. In addition, Wild would have had a good sense of international tastes, as Cooke & Sons had been exporting designs since the 1879 Sydney International Exhibition (where it had exhibited with Jeffrey & Co. and Carlisle & Clegg). Wild remained with the firm for forty-six years, producing a full range of styles, including traditional designs, pictoral friezes and swirling poppy patterns that, like chrysanthemum designs, were a characteristic motif around 1900.

Large, bold pictorial and floral friezes were new to wallpapers in the 1890s. At the beginning of 1895 the *Journal of Decorative Art* declared Messrs. Sanderson to 'hold an unchallenged position' in producing friezes, having 'mastered the secret as none of their competitors have done'. A range of techniques were used: block-printed outlines with stencil infills, and graduated stencil effects, most probably those done with the aerograph, an airbrush from which the spray-gun developed, and described in 1905 as 'a departure of the last few years'. The same report credits Harold Sanderson with 'discernment and artistic perception' and holds him responsible for the change in taste from aesthetic tertiary colours to papers 'printed in a bright, sparkling, yet harmonious colour note upon which the public seized with avidity'.[13]

Colouring was not a minor matter; then as now, it often defined fashionable trends more than did the pattern. Sanderson's colour choices were highly influential in this respect:

a 1901 article commented that 'Messrs. Sanderson's colourings for some years past have given the lead to the paper-hangings market, and they have had the compliment paid to them of many imitations.'[14] Earlier still, in 1897, the perfection of surface-wash printing by machine at Chiswick had finally produced the transparent or translucent tones that William Morris had sought, and which had only been achieved by Jeffrey & Co. for hand-prints. Sanderson's machine-printed variety was deemed to provide 'broken tints' with effects 'far ahead of anything in opaque printing'. In addition, the product was 'very hygienic, being hard on the surface and non-absorbent'. The colours in these and all other papers were by now pigments that, despite their additional cost, were 'permanent for all practical purposes'.[15] Sanderson had also been offering a woven wallcovering produced in 'permanent shades' for some years before 1904, when it was remarked that the call for it 'shows no sign of diminishing'.[16] This wallcovering was Fab-Ri-Ko-Na, made by H. B. Wiggin's Sons Co. in Bloomfield, New Jersey, USA.

The introduction of an American-made product to the Sanderson range might possibly have been the result of contacts made by Mr S. Loewenthal, who had been a travelling salesman 'on country ground' in Britain some years prior to 1890 and was listed as the company's foreign representative by 1901. (He may have travelled widely: it appears that Sanderson products were exported to South Africa before the outbreak of the second Boer

*Left* This surface-printed and aerograph-stencilled wallpaper of *c.* 1905 was inspired by a leather paper, but at 5*s.* per piece would have been much less expensive than leathers.

*Opposite, top left* Illustrated with a Sanderson frieze, this 1904 advertisement for W. H. S. Lloyd of New York City also notes its role as sole agent for the designs of Wm Woollams & Co., which Sanderson had acquired in 1901, and of Anaglypta, which Sanderson offered through the WPM.

*Opposite, top right* An aerograph-stencilled Sanderson frieze, no. 40101, *c.* 1902–4.

*Opposite, below* Detail of 'The Hillington Hunt Frieze' by Harry Watkins Wild, from a *c.* 1904 gouache sketch on tracing paper.

*Overleaf* A section of Wild's design for 'The Hillington Hunt Frieze'.

War in 1899, as company minutes refer to the restoration of this trade after the signing of the Treaty of Vereenig at the end of May 1902.) Certainly Loewenthal would have dealt with W. H. S. Lloyd Co., who was the sole Sanderson agent in the United States from at least about 1903, and in Canada from 1905. Lloyd's clients at this time included the Herter brothers, the influential interior decorators whose work for the Vanderbilts and other members of the American aristocracy is well documented.[17] Among the invoices from Lloyd to the Herters are two of December 1904 for 'The Hunting Frieze', comprising four panels designed by Harry Watkins Wild for Sanderson that had featured prominently at a trade exhibition earlier that year. These panels, of which four sets were ordered at a total cost of $32, were for the billiard room of Mrs McCann, undoubtedly Helena McCann, the Woolworth heiress who married her husband Charles in 1904 and resided with him at 4 East 80th Street in New York City.[18] Lloyd included several other Sanderson friezes in its advertisements, including landscapes, nursery themes and a pattern called

'The Titmouse Frieze'.[19] Given their often pictorial content, which attracted the attention of passers-by, the friezes were prominently featured during this period, whether at the trade fairs where Sanderson exhibited on a regular basis, in editorial features, or in advertisements, which the firm began to issue in the 1890s. Sanderson friezes were often paired with a machine-printed filling to reduce the cost to the builder's or decorator's eventual customer. By the early twentieth century an alternative that was simpler to hang was also developed, being a filling with an integral upper pattern, which would later be known as a 'crown' paper.[20] But there is no mistaking that friezes were *the* thing, a position they were to hold for several decades more, albeit by changing with the times.

ENGLISH HAND BLOCKED FRIEZE

Cable Address
"Intervene," New York

**W. H. S. LLOYD CO.** IMPORTERS OF

**ENGLISH, FRENCH AND JAPANESE WALL HANGINGS**

Sole Representatives in this Country of the Relief Decoration "ANAGLYPTA."

GRASS CLOTH, FIBRE PAPER— 26 East 22d Street, NEW YORK
FIGURED, STRIPED AND PLAIN

Sole Agents in U. S. for the well-known English lines of A. SANDERSON & SONS, WM. WOOLAMS and ANAGLYPTA

THE RILLINGTON HUNT. FRIEZE.

# The 'Mecca of Paperdom'

¶ Sanderson is sole agent for Gilmour doors by at least 1906.

¶ In 1907 the Sanderson brothers are declared to have 'the finest set of showrooms to be seen in London connected with the wall-paper business'.

¶ The sole agency for Tekko is held by the firm from 1909–13; thereafter the Chiswick factory prints Sanderson designs on plain Tekko grounds.

¶ In 1910 the company takes over the production of nursery friezes by Cecil Aldin and John Hassall.

¶ In 1911 Harold develops and patents two important technical advances in wallpaper manufacture.

¶ Sanderson acquires Charles Knowles & Co. in 1913; the Berners Street showroom is expanded in the same year.

¶ Sanderson introduces 'Post Impressionist' papers in 1913.

¶ The firm's supply of Japanese papers is expanded with the purchase of remaining stock from Rottman & Co. in 1914.

¶ The production of fancy box papers begins in 1914.

¶ John Sanderson dies in March 1915.

¶ A textile-printing factory is established at Uxbridge in 1919, producing Sanderson's own range of fabrics, which had been commission-printed since 1914.

¶ In 1919 the paint factory of Messrs Casson & Co. in Kensal Road, London, is purchased and the Berners Street showroom is expanded again.

¶ Arthur Bengough Sanderson is described as 'the creator of the greatest distributing house in decorative materials'.[1]

Stylistically speaking, the period between 1905 and 1920 is often regarded as a quiet interlude during which Edwardian propriety and the tragic effects of the First World War combined to produce little that was new but much that was pretty. While there were many traditional patterns issued by A. Sanderson & Sons during these years, it was also a period during which the company pressed forward: expanding its showroom, developing new techniques in Chiswick, and offering up innovative designs and products. For these efforts the firm was awarded several prizes, including the Grand Prix and a gold medal at the Franco-British Exhibition held in London in 1908, the Grand Prix at Turin in 1911 and a gold medal at a further international exhibition held in Amsterdam in 1920. The press, too, continued to heap praise – and occasionally hyperbole – on the collections issued by the firm. By 1914 one journalist was moved to ask, 'What is the secret of the continued and phenomenal growth of Messrs. Sanderson's business?' The answer: 'We must place first the capacity of the principals of the firm for organising; second, the character of Messrs. Sanderson themselves; they are happy in the possession of qualities which win the confidence of their customers. Then we must give an important place to their skill in producing papers that make an appeal to a wide constituency and a very varied taste.'[2] It is telling that the character of the partners was placed before the product itself, and this aspect of Sanderson's service – to its customers, its workers and the wallpaper industry – is where our story continues.

With what was said in 1907 to be the 'finest set of showrooms to be seen in London connected with the wall-paper business' at Berners Street, the firm continued to focus on providing products for the painter and decorator.[3] For customers who maintained retail premises, by 1909 the company was offering a music stand-like device used in Sanderson's own showroom and exhibition stands for displaying papers. Advertised as 'presentable in appearance', the stand was decorated in bronze and had a tripod base that could be raised or lowered to suit pattern lengths and create interesting groupings.[4] Sanderson was also sole agent for Canadian-made Gilmour doors from at least 1906, and in the following year 51 Berners Street was devoted to their display. With a five-ply softwood core faced in hardwood, Gilmours presaged the design of modern doors, and provided an affordable alternative to solid hardwood doors that, unlike the latter, did not shrink or warp. They were even available with different hardwoods on either side. By 1909 the Gilmour range include rotating 'anti-cyclone' doors, and in 1913 Sanderson showcased hygienic Gilmour hospital doors, 'made perfectly smooth, without nails, so there is no possible lodgment for dust, microbes or anything whatever', reporting that such doors had already been supplied to over a hundred hospitals.[5]

*Previous page* 'Eltham Vine', a mica-printed paper of 1909–13. Such Salubra papers from Switzerland, for which Sanderson held the sole agency, were referred to as 'Tekko brocades'.

*Below* Detail of a Japanese leather paper, possibly from the stock acquired by Sanderson from Rottmann & Co. in 1914. By this time Sanderson's own production of leather papers was said to be without rival.

*Opposite* Very similar to the design that won a gold medal at the Franco-British exhibition in 1908, 'The Cedar Tree and Peacock Chintz' was designed by Louis Stahl in the same year. Its printing required 46 blocks to create 150 colours, with an unusually large design repeat of nearly 2 metres.

The "Farm Yard" Frieze by Cecil Aldin.   2/2 per yd.   19½ in. wide.   Plain extension, 8d. per yd.

The "Noah's Ark" Frieze by John Hassall   2/2 per yd.   19½ in. wide.   Plain extension, 8d. per yd.

*Above* To suggest hand-painting, these blocked and stencilled friezes of 1911 ran for 35 feet (10.67 metres) before the design repeated. Plain insertions could extend the length still further.

Variations of the John Hassall 'Noah's Ark Frieze', which was also sold in New York by W. H. S. Lloyd, were available from Sanderson into the 1930s.

Meanwhile, the range of paints on offer expanded. Sanderson held sole agency for Paripan enamel and varnish, manufactured by Messrs Randall Bros; these products had 'already secured a very large market' by late 1906.[6] A year later the Wal-Pa-Mur sales agency for London and the Home Counties came to Berners Street. Branded to suggest the WPM, initially the Wal-Pa-Mur paints were water-based 'Hollins Distemper', named after the WPM's Hollins paper mill in Darwen, where the product was developed in 1906. The distemper had 'taken a great hold on the public taste' by 1910, by which time it had been 'tested and improved (by Mr Fred Jones)' and was 'now in an almost perfect condition'.[7] The manufacture of oil-based paint had also commenced under the same brand name, which evolved into 'Walpamur' soon thereafter; it continues to be produced under Orica Australia Ltd.[8] As for Sanderson's own paints, its 'Chiswick White – non-poisonous' variety was well-known by late 1912.[9] In 1919 Sanderson advertised Kingston flat varnish, flat white japan (matt-finish enamel) and, soon thereafter, Durolave, a water-based emulsion. In the same year, Sanderson purchased the paint factory of Messrs Casson & Co. in Kensal Road, London. After the First World War the firm also sold paintbrushes, among them stippling brushes 'constructed of the best materials upon a new principle without wood, save for the handle'.[10]

To serve its customers further, the company continued to extend its wallcoverings range, catering to every taste from conservative to modern. Its designers during this period were named as H. W. Batley, Beck, Entwistle, Labrane, Osborne, Pearce, Petremant, Shelton, James Thomas and Vivian, those whose names were cited in full being freelance designers. In addition to its own designs and products, in 1909 Sanderson obtained the sole agency for Tekko, keeping it until 1913, after which plain Tekko grounds were supplied to the Chiswick factory for embossing. This product, created by the long-established Salubra company (which still operates in Switzerland today), introduced lustrous, silk-like oil-colour papers to the market in 1901. In 1910 Sanderson obtained the Cecil Aldin and John Hassall nursery friezes originally produced by Lawrence & Jellicoe. The Hassall designs acquired by Sanderson at the time included the 'Nursery Rhyme' series, which was sold through Liberty & Co. By 1911 Aldin and Hassall's contribution to the Sanderson line included papers with sporting themes.[11]

With the acquisition of Charles Knowles & Co. in 1913, C. J. Knowles, Jr became a Sanderson salesman, supporting continued production from Knowles's rollers and blocks. Early in 1914 numerous Japanese leather papers were bought by Sanderson at the closure of Rottmann & Co. By then the price of a roll or panel of paper ranged from 1*s.* to 30*s.*, about £4 to £120 today, an exceptionally wide price spectrum reflecting Sanderson's many different manufacturing methods, styles and external sources of papers. Opponents of the WPM had claimed that the

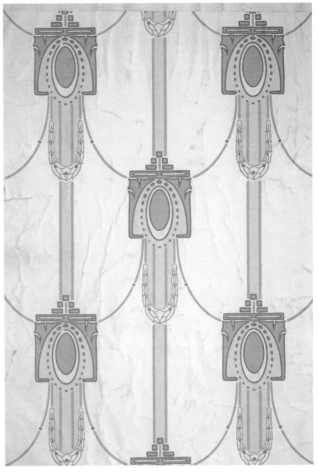

formation of the combine would reduce the selection of available wallcoverings, compared to the enormous variety offered by independent firms in the late nineteenth century. Sanderson's continued provision of a wide and diverse range did much to assuage these fears.

With forty customers easily accommodated simultaneously in the Berners Street showroom after 1907, this 'Mecca of paperdom' into which the 'numerous fashionables' poured, allowed the partners to 'feel the pulse of the public taste' and 'apprehend the drift of things'.[12] Yet by 1911 it was deemed too small, resulting in new showrooms at 51–52 Berners Street by 1913. Within months one room was modified to contain racks for show-rolls, since some customers preferred this type of display. Alterations to the front of 53–55 were considered in 1915 but abandoned, it being a difficult time for the trade. This was a loss to posterity, since the proposed alterations included architectural suggestions from C. F. A. Voysey, whose 1902 Chiswick factory is now a listed building.[13]

For customers who could not make the journey to London, the small 'travelling books' for the painting and decorating trade continued to be updated. From about 1908 cut-out borders were inserted over the 'plains' in the pattern books to demonstrate their effect. New in 1913 was 'a charming little folder containing three coloured illustrations of [Sanderson] designs…a page being left for the decorator to insert his own name and business address'.[14] These miniature pattern books supplemented the

*Above left* In 1914 Sanderson produced a small booklet, illustrated by Val Prince, from which comes this music room richly decorated with various Sanderson products: paints, a ceiling paper, a faux-mosaic paper frieze and soirette panelling embossed to resemble textured silk.

*Above right* Epitomising both the neo-Biedermeier and neo-Empire fashions of *c.* 1905–18, this block-printed paper was supplied by Sanderson to the Hyde Park Hotel, London, in about 1907.

*Overleaf* These two block-printed wallpapers were among several designed in 1907 by C. F. A. Voysey for Sanderson. 'Fool's Parsley' (*left*) was reproduced as a hand screen-print in the late 1960s; 'The Cleves' (*right*) was revived for the Sanderson 150th anniversary collection, Spring 2010.

*Above left* This is possibly the rose tree design by John Cantrill of Manchester that featured in a Sanderson 1909 exhibition stand demonstrating a novel application of a crown decoration. The rose tree was carefully cut out and applied to a calendered crêpe-paper ground. Its stipple effect was block-printed in gum tragacanth, a viscous, water-soluble natural gum used as a traditional binder for block-printers' colours.

*Above right* This surface roller-printed paper is very like one exhibited at the 1908 Franco-British Exhibition in London. It typifies the Edwardian taste for dainty trellis and bouquet patterns.

*Left* Issued in 1912, 'Windsor Castle' was machine-printed on textured paper to simulate tapestry. Almost continuously available until 1939, it was revived for the American market, selling there from 1952 until 1968.

*Opposite* 'Wisteria' and 'Rose and Convolvulus', crown-type filling and frieze papers, appeared in Sanderson's booklet *A Few Decorative Suggestions for Season 1911*.

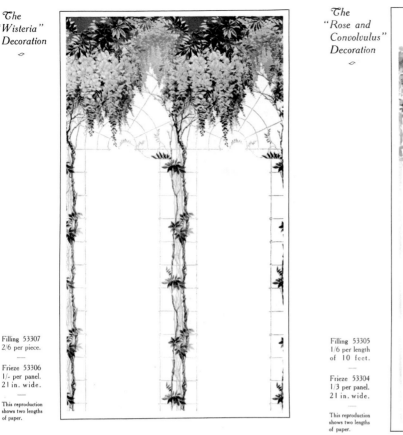

The "Wisteria" Decoration

Filling 53307
2/6 per piece.

Frieze 53306
1/- per panel.
21 in. wide.

This reproduction
shows two lengths
of paper.

The "Rose and Convolvulus" Decoration

Filling 53305
1/6 per length
of 10 feet.

Frieze 53304
1/3 per panel.
21 in. wide.

This reproduction
shows two lengths
of paper.

advertisements that the company placed with increasing frequency from 1901, and the illustrated booklets produced by the firm from 1911 onwards.

Due to the outbreak of war and consequent loss of nearly all of its trade to the Continent and three-quarters of its 'colonial trade', Sanderson's advertising ceased and no new pattern books were issued in 1915. Nevertheless, in 1916, despite the scarcity of materials and labour, twelve new books appeared in response to slightly improving sales at home and abroad. These books were reused until 1920, with additions of a few new patterns each year. Such privations notwithstanding, the Berners Street showroom was renovated soon after the armistice of November 1918. Settles by Ambrose Heal were introduced later that year, and shortly afterwards even a tea-room for customers and the public was considered , but abandoned.[15]

Throughout these years, amid the expected stripes, florals, chintzes and damask-like patterns offered by Sanderson, were many 'crown decorations' (a term that appears to have been agreed upon in 1906 to describe fillings with integral upper patterns). The Adams style, by no means newly revisited, was nevertheless declared a 'decided vogue' in 1908.[16] Victorian trellises were revived and note was made generally of the 'elegance and daintiness of papers' at this time.[17] Oriental influences became more evident, as in 1910, when a large Japanese screen 'attracted much attention and admiration'.[18] Other expressions

of this trend ranged from a renewed interest in Japanese leather papers – said in 1912 to be masterpieces and to have nothing in common with the old familiar types[19] – to papers with Chinese lanterns hung amid huge, bulbous flowers. Soon thereafter, one journalist noted that 'tapestry effects [are] coming back to us in increasing volume.'[20] The tapestry effects complemented the increasing number of patterns based on embroideries, which had grown in popularity since the beginning of the century, particularly those derived from Jacobean crewelwork.

Despite the diversity of patterns offered by Sanderson in the opening decades of the twentieth century, the large landscape panels in an imitation-tapestry effect shown in 1911 and also available as an imitation leather, give a clue to the prevailing trends: patterns were becoming more robust, naturalistic and three-dimensional. The same emphasis on three-dimensionality can be seen in the beaten-copper panels mentioned in the *Journal of Decorative Arts* in May 1909, for which Sanderson was sole agent, and, in 1912, 'the clever little mouldings of wood-backed compos' that provided a decorative 'wrought-iron surface with raised nail heads' to accentuate leather effects.[21]

Texture in particular was a defining element of this period. Many of the textured wallpapers were unpatterned or with small tone-on-tone effects, predating the development of such papers by the Bauhaus by over twenty years. The 1907 showroom entrance walls had been hung with a self-coloured 'oatmeal'-

*Above left* With a heavily embossed deep yellow ground overprinted with gold and opaque beige and cream pigments, this *c.* 1913 wallpaper simulates a Renaissance velvet. Its design would have been overseen by Mr Labrane, then the senior designer at Chiswick.

*Above right* A detail from a Sanderson pattern book showing canvas-textured papers arranged into panels with bordered surrounds, the downward sections of which were called 'stiles'.

*Right* All-over leafy patterns were often called 'tapestry' papers, and Sanderson produced similar designs as leather papers. This example dates from *c.*1912–20. Like the crewelwork-inspired pattern above, such designs remained popular well after the First World War.

*Opposite* A Val Prince illustration from the 1914 Sanderson booklet *Decorative Art*, this interior sets off texture-embossed 'plain' panels with decorative stile papers and a faux gold-leaf frieze band.

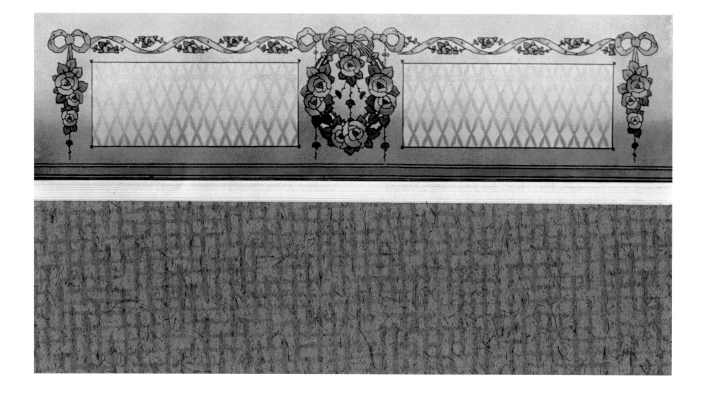

textured ingrain, above which was a deep frieze of the sort prevalent at the time. However, simple 'Bordered Papers' were gaining ground. Even at the 1908 Franco-British Exhibition, a showcase for Sanderson's 'distinctly eclectic' offerings, dominant features were panels filled with canvas-textured paper, 'plain but for the borders all around', with downward sections called 'stiles' between the panels.[22] By 1909 these 'panellings' included a good range of coarse scrim, very coarse-textured papers (including patterned 'oatmeals'), ingrains and Art-Ko-Na cloths.[23] In the following year Sanderson attracted comment for 'a kind of grass cloth' with designs printed on it, other semi-plains suggestive of embroidery textures or threaded work, coarse-string and linen textures, and plain silk-fibre effects. Even moirés were described as 'texture grounds, as they depend for effect on texture'.[24] By the spring of 1911, within the twelve books issued were a new 'water effect', as well as silk flocks, more imitation grass cloths, ingrains (which 'will not give up the ghost') and embossed papers, one on a ground 'that is quite new to us, namely, imitation basket work'.[25] Later in 1911 new pebble-embossed papers appeared.[26] Such rugged textures, together with linens (both plain and printed) and 'a special new "leather" being made at Chiswick', which was introduced early in 1913 at 25s. per piece, provided the backbone of the ranges until about 1920.[27]

Two major developments contributed to the variety of such textural effects. The first was the introduction of more cloths from Wiggin's Fab-Ri-Ko-Na Mill in New Jersey. These fabrics, especially those woven as wallcoverings, were promoted in North America as 'Craftsman products' by Gustav Stickley and offered genuine modernity to the public, being colourfast to light, simple to apply, washable with a damp sponge and affordable.[28] The

second development was two new techniques invented by Harold Sanderson and patented in 1911.[29] One produced a wallpaper formed of two materials glued together by embossing rollers; the other combined printing and embossing rollers in exact register. Both were of great benefit to the industry thereafter. At Chiswick, they accounted for the 'boom' in textured papers, such as those with basketwork, tweed, leather and skin effects, the leather and skin effects often accompanied by 'a narrow embossed border, most cleverly designed and treated in colour and metal'.[30]

A related development under Harold's supervision was the production of fancy box papers – both those for covering the outsides of boxes and those used for wrapping goods – which were in production by October 1914. This business boomed despite, or rather because of the war, since most box papers had previously been imported from Germany. By 1916 they warranted a separate department, which sold not only various textured, leather and skin papers, but also pictorial box-tops and special packaging for products such as John Knight's Pure Soaps.

The pigments for these and other products were always under review, and in mid-1913 the Board decided that their pattern books should declare that the products were 'fast to light'.[31] Colouration itself denoted modernity, whether in 1909, when a 'daring piece of colouring … in a broad stripe, purple and green, broken at recurring intervals with a pattern on a broken white circle of green and blue' was described as 'singularly successful', or in 1911–12, when patterns with black backgrounds caught journalists' eyes.[32] Paving the way for the latter trend was the striking combination of black and white in the 'Chequers' border, which received attention from 1908 to

*Opposite and left* Two of the 1911 range of textured papers made possible by Harold Sanderson's perfection of machine-embossing. Each has a block-, stencil- and aerograph-patterned frieze designed by George R. Rigby, who specialised in stencil patterns. The end and centre ornaments were supplied separately, one centre costing 2*s*.6*d*., as much as an entire piece of the filling.

*Below left* Announcing Sanderson's 'fast-to-light-wallpapers', this advertisement was issued in journals such as *The Studio* from January 1914 onwards.

*Below* 'A novel bathroom scheme' depicted by Val Prince in the 1914 Sanderson booklet includes a machine-printed faux-marble filling with applied stencilled upper panels and borders in 'The Chequers', which had been available since 1908.

1910; such borders were praised for their adaptability, since they were supplied separately and applied at the discretion of the decorator.[33] The colouring of all these designs reflected an awareness of developments in European arts and interiors, whether the brilliant tones associated with the Ballets Russes, Atelier Martine or Fauvist paintings, or the Successionists' taste for black-and-white effects. Clearly up-to-date in this respect, Sanderson's introduction of four 'Post Impressionist' papers in late 1913 followed rapidly on the heels of the opening of Roger Fry's Omega Workshops in London.[34] Of these papers it was said that 'their attractions lie in a certain archaic quality of drawing, and a "rude" taste in colour, which has a touch of the barbaric strength about it'.[35] The same colourings and approach to design can be found in the printed textiles that Sanderson began to develop in January 1914.

The addition of textiles to the firm's extensive product range was at first tentative, with designs being produced by outside printers, but it was in full swing by the end of the war, when land at Uxbridge was acquired for a textile-printing factory. The range was named Eton Rural Cretonnes, changing by spring 1922 to Eton Rural Fabrics. By 1919 Harold Nightingale – who had joined the firm c. 1900 and some five years later was managing a wallpaper factory in France that the Sandersons owned[36] – was in charge of the cretonne factory. The new Uxbridge facility included a laboratory, like the one already well-established at Chiswick. Since c. 1900 the chemist at the Chiswick laboratory had been Dr Edith Humphrey, the first woman 'to pass the B.Sc. Examination of London and Zurich' and quite possibly the first female chemist in the textile and wallpaper industry.[37]

During this period the partners were said to have led the way in providing for the welfare of their workforce. Support was given to a wide range of activities; for example, prior to the First World War there was an annual concert given at Berners Street by 'Messrs Sanderson's Orchestra'. At Chiswick, and later Uxbridge, provisions for the safety, health and recreation of employees were well-funded.[38] During the First World War the company guaranteed jobs for all servicemen when they returned, and looked after their families in the meantime. This policy was instigated by John Sanderson, whose death in March 1915 was perhaps the greatest wartime loss to the company. He was remembered as 'a kind-hearted, generous and well-liked man', whose 'philanthropy was well-known and one contemporary remarked that he had known him assist people who had no real claim on him of any sort "not with the odd sovereign or two…but with substantial sums"'.[39] He is also credited with formulating a Sanderson marketing policy that remained in place for the rest of the century. His approach focused on aiding the decorator by issuing illustrations of completed rooms, and on paying close attention to the trends gleaned from tradespeople and their customers during visits to the showroom.

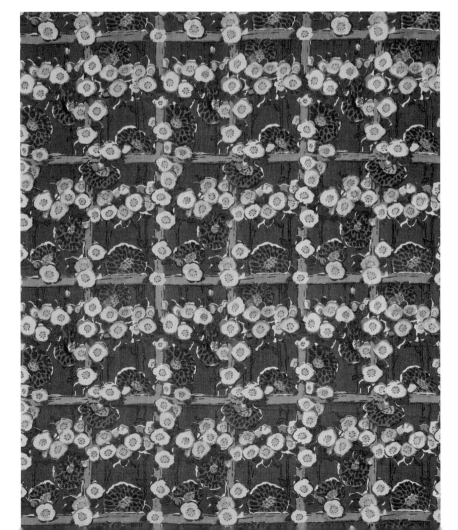

*Opposite* This surface-printed paper, with the rich colours and black ground that attracted the attention of journalists in 1911–12, is attributed to Charles Rennie Mackintosh.

*Left* Resembling designs in the 1913–15 'Post Impressionist' range, this textured cotton was roller-printed for Sanderson by Stead McAlpin in Carlisle. The order was placed in March 1918 for the following year, when Sanderson issued papers to match its cretonnes.

*Overleaf* Sections of 'The Phoenix Bird Decoration', attributed to Harry Watkins Wild, issued in 1919 and displayed at a trade fair in 1922. Further panels were then added until, in 1927, the entire set extended over 28 feet (8.5 metres) and required 311 blocks to print.

# *Towards 'Wallpaper Decoration'*

¶ The Sanderson textile-printing factory in Uxbridge is producing a full range of fabrics by autumn 1921.

¶ The Essex & Co. showroom is bought by Sanderson in 1923 and maintained until late 1939, during which time many of the early C. F. A. Voysey designs are successfully revived.

¶ Photogravure machine-printing of wallpapers begins at Chiswick in 1923; by 1924 the factory is able to machine-print up to twenty colours.

¶ In 1924 Arthur Bengough Sanderson becomes the holder of a Royal Warrant as Purveyor of Wallpapers and Paints to King George V. This is said to be the first Warrant granted for the supply of these products.

¶ Jeffrey & Co. becomes part of the WPM in 1924; Horace and Albert Warner immediately became designers at Chiswick; 53 Berners Street is given over to the 'Jeffrey Gallery' in 1926 and the designs, blocks (including those for Morris & Co.) and machines are sent to Chiswick a year later. 'The Persian', one of Jeffrey & Co.'s most famous patterns, is reissued in 1936.

¶ The agencies of two French mills, Zuber and Turquetil, are acquired from E. S. Theobald of Newman Street, London, between 1926 and 1928.

¶ Fire destroys the Chiswick factory in 1928. A new wallpaper factory is completed at Perivale by 1930. On a site covering eighty acres and with extensive facilities for sporting and social events, it is said to be the finest in the world. It remains in company hands until 1973.

¶ In 1929 Berners Street becomes part of the WPM. The WPM also takes over the Sanderson paint-making plant, which is developed into a WPM branch factory to serve the south of England.

¶ Collaboration with Disney Studios begins by 1930.

¶ In 1931 the existing arrangement with the American manufacturers Birge & Co. ends; Birge & Co. close its Berners Street showroom and assign the agency and stock of leather papers and scenic decorations to Sanderson.

¶ During 1931 and 1932 the Heffer & Scott wholesale and export business is transferred to Sanderson, who, having purchased a controlling interest in 1928, acquires the remaining assets in 1934.

¶ Arthur Bengough Sanderson retires in 1932, leaving 400 staff at Berners Street; Harold Sanderson retires in 1934, leaving twice that number at Perivale. The new chairman is Harold's son Ivan, who joined the firm in 1921.

¶ Morris & Co. goes into voluntary liquidation in 1940 and Sanderson buys the wallpaper business together with the rights to use the company name, acquiring blocks, logbooks and existing stock, including the entire contents of the Hanover Square showroom.

The oft-used phrase *le plus ça change, le plus c'est la même chose* accurately describes the story of Arthur Sanderson & Sons between 1920 and 1940. Although much *did* change in economic terms, the pace of design innovation, acquisitions and investment in the firm's technology and factories remained as vigorous as ever, despite the impact of the Depression mid-way through this period. Perhaps the greatest change came not as a result of the economy, but from the widening circulation of women's magazines, with their occasional inclusion of colour plates, and from the greatly increased role of women themselves in the design, promotion and selection of decorative products for interiors. *Homes & Gardens* was established in 1919 and *Ideal Home* in 1922, along with other short-lived publications aimed at a female readership, such as *Decoration (Beauty and the Home)*, published from 1930–*c*. 1934, which frequently included colour plates illustrating Sanderson products.

In 1930 a lecture was given at the Painters' Hall, London, by Mrs Grace Lovat Fraser. Her comments are worth repeating at the outset as they highlight the issues that informed Sanderson's provision of ever-more co-ordinated ranges, colourful cloths, inexpensive 'special effects' and advertisements aimed directly at the homeowner rather than the professional decorator.

Fraser was well qualified to speak to the professionals gathered on that occasion. Her experience included interior decoration, hand-printing fabrics and operating her own design advisory bureau; she was at the time also the editor of the magazine *Art and Industry*. Reminding her audience that women had become 'decoration conscious' since the Depression, she went on to point out that they 'have kept their habit of attention to detail, however, so that when they begin to worry out a scheme for the decoration of a given room, they plan it as a whole and not simply in terms of paint and paper'. As a result, the average woman 'will want someone who knows something about the right colours for different types of period decoration, who knows what happens to colour under artificial light, and will keep her from getting a room which is charming by daylight and like the wrath of God at night'. Noting that her queries from women showed that they wanted 'the new and the fresh' and 'have no use

*Previous page* Typifying the 1920s taste for simplified fruit patterns in bold colours with pronounced outlining, this example was machine-printed on textured paper.

*Above* A selection of surface-printed cottons, all issued as Eton Rural Fabrics in 1922–25, except the stripe, an Eton Rural Cretonne of 1919–22. The uppermost pattern was reissued in 2010.

*Opposite* Reflecting a change in its marketing policy, Sanderson appealed directly to primary consumers in this 1930 advertisement by Horace Taylor.

PUNCH, OR THE LONDON CHARIVARI.—March 26, 1930.

## THE SUNNIEST ROOM IN THE HOUSE !

When you decorate a dull room with a Sanderson Wallpaper you transform it. It is like pulling up the blinds on a sunny morning. The room which had the sulks now smiles, the room which was so dowdy and dreary is now the sunniest room in the house. The Sanderson Wallpaper Book shows you paper after paper which is a joy to look at, and will be a pleasure to live with. On no account have any decorating done until you have asked your decorator to show you this most inspiring book.

# SANDERSON WALLPAPERS

ARTHUR SANDERSON & SONS LTD., 52-55 BERNERS STREET, LONDON, W.I
6 & 7 Newton Terrace, Glasgow, C.3 ✿ 20 Rue des petits Champs, Paris

*Above* The Sanderson archive holds numerous logbooks containing photographic records of designs, some of which were never produced. This example, UX401, dates from 1927–28.

*Opposite* The metallised canvas ground of this *c.* 1926 machine-printed paper was produced at Chiswick using a photogravure machine; the pattern was then surface-printed using water-based emulsions. In 2010, as 'Primavera', this pattern was issued as part of the Sanderson 150th Anniversary collection as a fabric and wallpaper.

for the stereotyped or ordinary', she emphasised that her interest was in the woman of small means rather than those of wealth who could afford to consult 'the swell in his profession', and stressed that 'one of the most crying needs of the decorative profession to-day is the education of the youngsters' as apprentices.[1]

On many of these points Sanderson was ahead of the game, with its electrically lit showroom and papers coloured especially for such light, as well as its release of plates showing ideas for complete interiors, all prior to the war. During the inter-war years the firm also made originality in design a priority while striving to provide high-quality goods at reasonable prices and supporting informative and educative endeavours. This chapter focuses on these aspects of Sanderson's progress during this

period, although the firm's technical and business expansion is not to be overlooked.

The inter-war economy was to reduce many people to a more modest income, and Sanderson made every effort to adapt to its customers' the straitened circumstances. Although block-printing, stencilling and the occasional excursion into hand-painting were maintained throughout this period – the blocks on occasion being utilised to apply several colours at once – even these techniques were combined with machine effects. The care Sanderson expended on its cheaper lines was especially notable in 1923, when Harold Sanderson installed single-colour photogravure machines at Chiswick that had been purchased from the government still bearing the rollers used to print ration

cards during the First World War. The machines were first employed to produce canvas textures, then woodgrain papers, which were polished by hand and said to be the first on the world market; other effects followed, such as gold-leafing and dry-bronzing. By 1926 Sanderson's machine-printed papers included metalised canvases, mother-of-pearl effects created by embossing, new washable marble papers and an ever-widening range of woodgrain papers.[2] At this time the press also noted the firm's handmade cut-out crown and base borders, together with its hand-printed scenics and 'growths' (large motifs rising from the base border), but by 1930 it was Sanderson's textural papers and cut-out borders that were said to have revolutionised the wallpaper trade.[3]

The Chiswick factory was destroyed by fire in 1928; two years later, on eighty acres at Perivale, Middlesex, a new factory arose, 'the finest wall paper mill in the world'.[4] Block-printing and stencilling operations were maintained alongside the printing machines, which were soon to number thirty. Several of them were capable of printing twenty colours at one time, and the cut-outs were now done by electric pen.[5] Thereafter the 'astonishing range of machine-made corners, borders and other cut-outs' and the 'sound range of [low-priced] canvas effects' drew increasing attention; in 1932 it was noted that Sanderson's machine-printing had 'reached a stage of perfection at which only the practised hand can say with certainty whether the block

or the machine is responsible for a given design'.[6] Machine-printed flocks were perfected in 1935; a year later came an 'immensely effective range of new stipples, at so modest a price as to suggest that some method of machine stippling has been evolved', and 1938 saw the arrival of 'new plastic prints', meaning machine-made raised effects with a plaster-like printing medium.[7]

The surest signs that Sanderson understood its market were the changes in its advertising and promotional endeavours throughout the 1920s and 1930s. In 1921 the firm was praised for its 'wizards of display'; its stand at that year's Manchester National Exhibition was a striking departure from the 'Georgian' treatment created the year before for the Ideal Home Exhibition at Olympia, and received detailed coverage in the press: 'Consider a white rectangle coped with a flat black projecting cornice; the sides pierced by black arches edged with a tilelike stencil of alternate grey blue and grey green, bordered with black spots, and within each arch against the black hangings and lit by hidden lights, the most glowing drapings of coloured cretonnes one could conceive.'[8] This display method was similar to that used for the first stand devoted to Eton Rural Cretonnes at a textile trade show in London earlier that year.[9] The use of electric light anticipated the needs of Grace Lovat Fraser's perplexed readers. Although a Sanderson advertisement of the period states that its products were 'supplied only through the trade', it

Top left Scenic papers were promoted through Sanderson booklets, exhibition stands, sample-book lithos and advertisements, all of which in 1927–28 featured 'The Phoenix Bird Decoration' for which Walter Francis had created additional panels.

Top right Scenics were also shown off via the stage sets for Sanderson's own amateur dramatic society, here performing Katinka at the Fortune Theatre on Drury Lane in London, c. 1937.

Centre Sanderson's stand at the 1931 Ideal Home Exhibition, designed by Edward Newman, was praised for its complete room sets.

Left During the 1930s Sanderson offered a wide range of canvas-effect papers embellished with machine-made corners, borders and other cut-outs. The example shown here is from 1939.

Opposite Both of these wallpapers were illustrated in the JDA, no. 45094, the pinecone pattern (left) in January 1923 and the slow-motion surface-printed peacock pattern by Harry Watkins Wild (right) in October 1926. Both also display the range of grounds produced by photogravure printing.

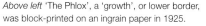

*Above left* 'The Phlox', a 'growth', or lower border, was block-printed on an ingrain paper in 1925.

*Opposite* 'Snow White and the Seven Dwarfs', a Sanderson Indecolor Fabric from at least 1938, had a matching wallpaper and companion frieze and border. Sanderson became a licensee for Disney fabrics in the early 1930s.

*Above right* John Hassall's design for this 1925 surface roller-printed cotton was registered in July 1922. The reverse is inscribed 'Norman Hartnell'.

*Below* This machine-printed Peter Pan paper, 1931, had stencilled cut-outs of fairies, to be positioned at the decorator's discretion.

was well understood by this time that many visitors were not tradesmen, but eventual customers.

Sanderson exhibited frequently. In the first half of 1922, for example, the firm was represented at the annual Manchester decorators' trade exhibition, the Ideal Home Exhibition, the Drapery, Textile and Women's Wear Exhibition, and the Women's Exhibition organised by the *Daily Express* at Olympia, among others. Although the company's stand at the Women's Exhibition was declared 'wholesale only', there was little doubt that the consumer was the real target of Sanderson's marketing efforts. Even in the exhibitions not containing 'women' in their titles, special features intended to make 'a direct appeal to feminine visitors' were evident.[10] At the Ideal Home Exhibition it was a 'soirette' paper chosen by Princess Mary for her bedroom.[11] An arched stand, similar to the one that had featured in the Manchester Home Exhibition display, was used for this show, although the rectangle now had a higher 'block' centrally placed on each side. The stand, like its predecessors, was designed by Edward Newman, art advisor to the firm from May 1919, whose 'severe simplicity' of form and 'cunning light' presaged much that would be seen at the 1925 'Art Deco' Exposition Internationale in Paris. He continued to design Sanderson stands until at least 1931, by which time the arches had evolved into fully-resolved room sets.[12] Clearly successful, the display concept was introduced at Berners Street by the following year, billed as 'an innovation at Sanderson's'.[13]

Sanderson also appealed directly to women through its nursery papers, which had become a consistent feature of the ranges before the war. These included a 'fairie' filling of 1923, in the style of Hassall, and delicately-drawn cut-outs issued a few years later, most probably in the wake of the 1924 silent-film version of *Peter Pan*. By 1931 these cut-outs were promoted in

conjunction with a scenic paper that depicted a cloudy sky above shallow banks of wild flowers.[14] (In the same 'plain' vein were the scenics with cut-out flying ducks, intended primarily for bathrooms.) Cretonnes were also supplied, some in the style of Will Kidd, who had designed the Eton Rural letterhead and tickets, and others by or after Hassall, whose 'parades' of children with wagons were by now well known.

What changed the children's range from an adjunct to a 'featured player' was the introduction of fabrics and papers based on Walt Disney characters. The working drawings featuring Mickey Mouse ('born' in late 1928) were shown in 1930 during the Duke of York's visit to the new Perivale factory. (He had visited Chiswick in 1924, when the firm had been granted the Royal Warrant as Purveyors of Wallpaper and Paint to HM George V – said at the time to be the first issued to a firm of wallpaper manufacturers.[15]) The Disney collaboration was clearly successful. Disney characters such as Mickey and Goofy (who was introduced in 1932), scamper across a filling illustrated in 1938; another filling (priced 2s.6d. per roll, about £6 today) with frieze and stiles showing Snow White and the Seven Dwarfs was issued in the same year. 'All these', it was reported, 'will be popular, if only because the children will delight in having their film heroes and heroines on their own walls'.[16] There were also companion fabrics in most cases; that for Snow White featured in a Sanderson 1938 advertising campaign that appealed directly to women by stressing the washproof and sun-resistant qualities of Sanderson Indecolor Fabrics – an appellation introduced in 1937 – and the benefit to health produced by opening the blinds and curtains in the nursery.[17]

Advertising by this time had also shifted its focus from the trade to the final customer. For example, the well-known cartoonist, poster artist and illustrator Horace Taylor provided a series of vivid images to accompany an already established 'Ask Your Decorator' campaign. His colour campaign, begun by 1930, reflected the Sanderson view that 'a gloomy horizon for international trade has not checked the forward policy [which] has been to meet depression with enterprise'. 'That', added a journalist in recording the Sanderson approach, 'is the way to get rid of depression.'[18] (Nevertheless, by the spring of 1932 Sanderson's Parisian showroom, managed throughout the 1920s by one Cronier, had closed, and its address was removed from the showroom listings in the 'Ask Your Decorator' advertisments.[19]) The company's outlay on advertising was boosted to £6,000 by 1931, when there was an additional £1,000 already set aside specifically for advertising Eton Rural Fabrics (as they were called from 1922 to 1936) in women's journals.[20] Parallel initiatives to aid a customer's choice came in the revived sale 'for a modest fee' of booklets intended to be passed to clients by the decorator – whose name could now be printed on the front – 'a great opening for publicity of a most judicious kind'.[21] A subtle

but telling acknowledgment of the active role of the consumer appears in the media response to a 1935 Sanderson booklet, *Interiors for To-day*, at a time when booklets were still considered a medium by which decorators could 'push' the use of wallpaper. With twenty-eight illustrations, twenty in full colour, it was judged to be 'beautifully produced, packed with sound and very practical ideas for rooms, and represents as effective a temptation to decorate as we have yet seen'.[22]

Innovations in the pattern books included the consistent insertion of illustrations from about 1924. By the mid-1930s these embraced both line drawings and 'litho illustrations' (or colour plates, still called 'lithos' today whatever their means of production). In 1938 clear acetate sheets carrying sketches of an interior were laid over textured papers, while in 1939 the books included a 'very helpful and ingenious device' in which 'certain of the fillings in the pattern books are over printed with sketches in flat colour of furniture, carpet and accessories, giving more than a hint of the completed scheme'.[23] However, most ingenious of all was a device noted as part of the display mounted at a trade fair in Brighton in 1937: 'the famous "press button" machine, which brings to view a seemingly endless range of interiors in water colour, to the great delight of the many visitors to whom any exhibition is first of all an entertainment'.[24]

New and fresh ideas in design were abundant in the inter-war ranges. The cretonnes presented in 1921 made an immediate

*Above left* The Sanderson wallpaper books for 1938 included this one, entitled *Plain Tints, Textures, Stipples, Rough Cast, Etc*, in which illustrations appeared on clear acetate sheets.

*Above right* In the 1939 'plains' wallpaper book, decorative schemes were suggested by overprinting directly onto the paper, which in this example is a 'plastic print', machine printed with a plaster-like medium.

*Opposite, left* One of a series of nine advertisements for 1930–34 designed by Horace Christopher Taylor, who was then a lecturer at the Chelsea School of Art.

*Opposite, right* This page from a *c*. 1928 Sanderson pattern book illustrates the type of lower-priced papers described by one *JDA* journalist in 1931 as reminiscent of watercolours on vellum.

*Overleaf* Two Eton Rural Fabrics of 1929. The pattern on the left is by Mea Angerer, who in early 1928, then still resident in Vienna, was paid £40 for four designs for this range.

impact, with a wallpaper border in the same tones and a 'plain' filling.[25] The cretonnes at this time were of de-sized Egyptian cotton, printed by surface-roller with 'magnificent jazz designs, stripes, and broken arrangements of orange and black, glimmering blue and gold, and jade, and rich crimson, treated with all the harmonious freedom and abandonment which is jazz'.[26] By 1922 the Eton Rurals were said to be so widely known as to need no introduction.[27] Vivid 'futuristic' colourings remained dominant, even in the more traditional styles, such as the 'Jacobeans' (said to be appropriate for the country), until about 1930, when colourations began to be less saturated. This trend was especially apparent in the 'shadow prints', warp-printed cloths introduced in 1931, for which a spinning and weaving complex was in operation at Uxbridge by 1934.[28] Modernist designs especially suited such fabrics; papers, too, showed more abstract, angular or geometric treatments in increasingly warm, soft shades.[29] Having made every possible clever use of borders, cut-outs, stiles, scenics and growths, Sanderson papers were next designed to be hung sideways. 'Horizontalism is everywhere,' announced one journalist in 1936, noting, too, that 'subtleties of contrast in tone, texture and colour will lend a new interest and…will emphasise the tendency, in the application of wallpaper, away from mere "paperhanging," and towards "wallpaper decoration".'[30]

To serve an enterprise now so large that in 1936 its worldwide business demanded that 2,000 orders and deliveries were handled in just one day,[31] Sanderson maintained three separate design studios at Berners Street, the Perivale wallpaper factory and Uxbridge, where the presence of designers was first noted in January 1927. The sole designer at Uxbridge in early March 1928 was Mea Angerer, who had trained at the Weiner Werkstätte and had come to England specifically to work in the Uxbridge studio, where she remained until April 1929, after which she became a freelance designer. From August 1928 she was joined by a Miss Thomas, possibly a relative of Barton Thomas who was head designer there throughout the 1930s. At Perivale the large studio under Walter Francis employed fourteen designers in 1932 and a further ten up to 1938; among these was Harry Watkins Wild, whose last design was logged in early March 1939.[32] Outside designers were also used, including the Haward Studio,[33] Percy Bilbie and Cecil H. Judge, who after training at Watford Art College had joined the Sanderson studio (possibly as part of the scheme established by Harold Sanderson that allowed art students a place for six or eight weeks at Perivale) and by the mid-1930s was also a freelance designer.[34]

Alongside the innovative designs for fabric and wallpaper during this period, one cannot pass over the paints and other decorators' supplies sold by Sanderson. In 1921 these included a transparent wood filler 'of real merit', Easilit blow lamps invented by Mr Yates,[35] and, in 1923, the Bernstoff electric torch, also for burning-off purposes. In the same year the firm

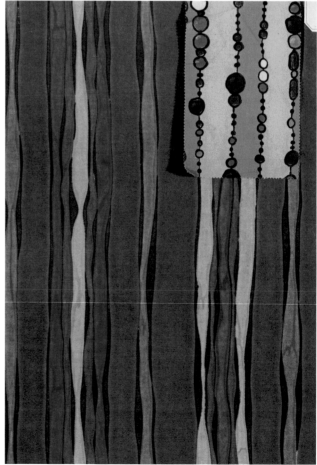

*Opposite* Two early examples from the Eton Rural range, dating from 1921–22 and employing designs attributed to the Silver Studio. All were surface-machine printed on 31 inch-wide cotton.

*Above* Two warp-printed reversible woven fabrics, the lower one *c.* 1933 and made by an outside weaver for Sanderson. The upper example was woven at Uxbridge in 1937; it remained available until 1953.

*Right* A surface-printed cotton designed by Harry Watkins Wild in 1929. It remained available until 1947.

*Above* This illustration of a model room at Berners Street, showing horizontally hung striped wallpaper, was incorporated into a 1936 advertisement by Notley. Stripes, woodgrains and other 'plain' papers contributed greatly to the sale in the previous year of over 100 million rolls of wallpaper by British manufacturers.

*Left* Photogravure printing, introduced by Harold Sanderson in 1923, was often used to create woodgrain papers, as shown in this Sanderson standbook of 1938. The 'Leaping Hounds' design displayed here is probably by one Southey, noted as a specialist in-house designer for gravure and embossing machines.

*Overleaf* Three Eton Rural Fabrics dating from 1933 and (*top*) 1935. All incorporate what was described as a 'modern ground' and sold relatively cheaply, for 1*s.*4*d.* to 1*s.*8*d.* per yard.

presented Sanstonia Stone Surface[36] and, in 1928, Durolave Santique, which created a cracked or crocodile-skin effect, together with the Durolave Portable Spraying Plant for nitro-cellulose lacquers as well as other paints.[37] A 'Lightening Stripper' was shown in Brighton in 1937, as were the Easilit lamps, each noted as having 'its own place in the affections of painters'.[38]

Nor can one overlook the Sanderson brothers themselves. Arthur Bengough Sanderson retired in 1932, leaving 400 staff at Berners Street and a reputation as a skilful negotiator who believed that work should be a labour of love. Ivan Sanderson (1899–1968), who had joined the firm in 1921 and taken over as Uxbridge fabric production manager in 1925, became chairman in early October 1934, on the retirement of his father, Harold Sanderson. Aside from his achievements in design and technology, Harold was also remembered as an avid supporter of design education. From his training of young women alongside young men at Chiswick and Perivale, to his underwriting of an RSA travelling bursary for art masters in 1934, he was a firm believer in the necessity of art for industry. Day visits from art schools

were encouraged, establishing a Sanderson tradition that was to be maintained for the rest of the century. Harold also endowed a training scheme for young designers that came into being after the Second World War. Like his older brother John, Harold served on the executive board of the Royal Society of Arts, from 1932 until 1942, the last seven years as vice-president; the RSA minutes indicate his 'unprecedented success in securing fresh support for the society', having introduced well over 300 fellows since his election.[39]

*Below* Nancy McClelland, author of the pioneering 1924 work *Historic Wall-papers from Their Inception to the Introduction of Machinery*, was also an influential American decorator who established her own firm in 1922. She provided the design for this Knowles sanitary wallpaper in 1913, just prior to the firm's acquisition by Sanderson, who continued to produce the design for a number of years.

7

# Fresh Ideas, New Colours and Modern Designs

¶ From 1940 until 1950 no new Sanderson pattern books are issued, there being no papers available from 1942 until the end of 1945. Single-sheet samples are available from mid-1946.

¶ The Sanderson factories meanwhile engage in war work.

¶ In May 1945 they make a substantial contribution to the landmark Exhibition of Historical & British Wallpapers held at the Suffolk Galleries, London.

¶ Sanderson is represented at the 'Britain Can Make It' exhibition held at the Victoria and Albert Museum in 1946, showing styles ranging from lush florals to papers with wood effects, figured spots and stripes.

¶ Uxbridge is extended and by 1950 is running 120 Jacquard looms in addition to those already weaving plain cloths.

¶ In 1951 Sanderson products appear in the Festival of Britain on London's South Bank, where the Royal Festival Hall is decorated exclusively with the company's papers.

¶ Imported textiles are introduced in 1951, and thereafter are obtained from Sweden, the United States, Italy and Germany among other countries; among the fabrics are those with designs by Picasso and Gio Ponti.

¶ Royal Warrants are granted to the firm in 1951 and 1955.

¶ Sanderson launches a series of exhibitions at Berners Street to showcase its new pattern books of 1952, 1954 and 1956.

¶ Dersine Fancy Papers, introduced in 1935, are highly successful during the 1950s and 1960s.

¶ In 1957 a programme of rebuilding begins at Berners Street, resulting in 'the world's most fabulous showrooms', designed by Slater & Uren, which open in 1960.[1]

¶ In 1960 Sanderson celebrates its centenary in its new building with an exhibition and special collections. Ivan Sanderson becomes the chairman of the WPM at the end of that year.

With the outbreak of war at the beginning of September 1939, everything changed for the decorative trades. At Sanderson, the 1940 wallpaper books were already being made, but by December 1941 the WPM stocks of raw paper had been exhausted. As printing ceased over the following months, the finished papers held by retailing painters and decorators also ran out. In effect, there were no wallpapers available in Britain from early 1942 until November 1945. Even when paper supplies were restored, these were insufficient, so the 1940 Sanderson pattern books remained in use until new sets could be issued in February 1950; meanwhile, only patterns in the cheaper ranges could be supplied. New designs on better paper were being printed by mid-1946 and issued to decorators in small loan books or as single-sheet samples (the latter becoming the standard practice), but the size of repeat was restricted to save wastage when matching patterns.

In mid-1947 it was reported that the industry was faced with 'an economic crash unparalleled in history', not only due to shortages of paper, but also of all types of paste and the threat of fuel shortages.[2] Prices, too were more than double their pre-war levels, partly due to the imposition of a purchase tax in late 1940 that mattered little until production began again, when it was set at one third of the purchase price. This issue so concerned manufacturers, decorators and many in the building trades that it was debated in Parliament, and, although the tax was subsequently reduced to 12½ per cent in 1953, it was never removed thereafter.[3] Uxbridge decorative fabrics, meanwhile, ceased to be manufactured in May 1942 and recommenced just over four years later, but the products were subject to rationing by coupon until 1949. Yet by 1960, when the company celebrated its centenary, Arthur Sanderson & Sons had launched a collection of some 4,500 designs in fabrics and wallpapers and had opened a new showroom and office building in Berners Street, 'which is probably the largest of its kind in the world'.[4] This chapter outlines how these remarkable achievements came about.

Idleness was the one thing the war did not allow. Along with other WPM factories, Sanderson's engaged in essential war work. Perivale produced, among other things, camouflage for 87,811 bomb doors on Wellington bombers and over 1.3 million fascias for tank and submarine control panels. At Uxbridge, land was leased to the army for an anti-aircraft station. Never a firm to miss an opportunity, Sanderson took advantage of the lack of restrictions on blackout and transparent protective window papers, which were exempted from purchase tax, and by 1941 was advertising a 'new kind of glass substitute' called Transolite, composed of a plain cellulose film coated on both sides with a protective transparent skin. By the end of the war over 54,000 yards had been made. War-damaged windows were common by late 1941, when Sanderson released Trellisand, a window replacement containing Transolite within a paned framework of

*Previous page* First produced in 1938, this fabric was available as a woven reversible-warp print, and, until 1966, as a print on both cotton satin and Sanderlin (pictured here), the Sanderson trade name for a permanent calendered-glaze finish pioneered at the Uxbridge Print Works. 'Swallows' was reissued in Spring 2010 as a print and wallpaper.

*Above* A book of hand-printed Dersine Fancy Papers of the late 1930s, showing patterns that were also offered after 1946.

*Opposite, left* Typical of the products shown by Sanderson at the 'Britain Can Make It' exhibition in 1946, G137/8, an eighteen-colour surface machine-printed fabric, bears a CC41 Utility label, used on Uxbridge fabrics during rationing.

*Opposite, right* An advertisement placed in *Punch* in May 1951.

*Above* A 'reminder' advertisement of the type placed by Sanderson during the late 1930s and the Second World War. Its designer, 'E. F.', has not been identified.

*Below* This Sanderson advertisement of 1949 includes illustrations of fabrics both newly designed and, on the left and right, 'Lupins' and 'Feathers', both dating from 1937.

lacquered compo-board, to be fixed with fillets or putty, or tacked to 'emergency woodwork'.[5] Sanderson fire-resistant and anti-condensation paints were also perfected and promoted during the war.

With shortages of decorative goods, advertising was curtailed, although before supplies ceased entirely a group of Sanderson room schemes highlighting 'the idea of controlled contrast' were circulated to magazine editors. Wallpapers were presented as a means of emphasising good features already present in an interior: a wooden door could be surrounded with a plain paper, while patterns were used to define areas, as in a lounge–dining room where the table was placed in a corner, set off with a dark-ground trellis pattern described, tellingly, as giving 'the air of a deliberate plan' rather than of 'a mere makeshift'.[6] Otherwise, under the banner 'Do You Remember?', a series of at least twenty-five advertisements reviewing the changes in wallpaper styles between the two wars, featuring military personnel in the foreground, were run until late 1944. Further 'reminder' advertisements, intended solely to keep the Sanderson name before the public, were allocated a budget in June 1945, and this was doubled in December 1946 to £5,000 (about £150,000 today).

However, by 1945 the sales vehicle that was to characterise the post-war period had already made its appearance. This was the exhibition, but it was far different from the trade fairs of the past. It emphasised informative presentations to give the public a

*Above* Hand screen-printing, which Sanderson used for specialists' papers from 1934, became widely mechanised after the Second World War. A 1950 example typifies the colouration of many post-war fabrics.

*Above* Thousands of box- and wrapping papers were printed at Perivale in the 1950s and 1960s, including this one for the English couturier Norman Hartnell, who designed the coronation gown worn by Queen Elizabeth II in 1953.

glimpse of the future and a taste for more colourful patterns. The first of these was the Exhibition of Historical & British Wallpapers, mounted in London in May 1945. Later described as 'a landmark in the development of postwar interior design [that] set the pace for the next few years',[7] the exhibition included room sets as well as proposals for modern papers, the latter contributed by at least 100 artists and designers. Sanderson papers were among the 500 examples of groups of stripes, metal papers, 'woods', florals and other styles that the organisers promised would be available after the war 'at prices within the reach of all'. Sanderson lent 30 per cent of the 224 historical examples, including a book of Morris patterns.[8] 'Marigold', from the Morris book, was included among the few new Sanderson patterns for 1946 as a monochrome design. As such, it sat happily among the condensed abstract florals and delicate contemporary sprigs and squiggles – most often light on a deep 'sugared-almond' or honeyed-wood-coloured ground – which had been introduced just before the war and characterised many designs for another five or so years after its end.[9]

In 1946, such patterns, and a selection from Sanderson's star, polka dot and trellis-based designs produced in the same 'white line' style, were exhibited at both the 'Britain Can Make It' exhibition, orchestrated by the Council of Industrial Design (CoID),[10] and at the *Daily Herald* Modern Homes exhibition, where Sanderson's contribution was said to be 'an effective

display, cleverly presented'.[11] The catalogue for the latter exhibition optimistically focused on the regeneration of Britain, showing plans for Loughton New Town and layouts for the six main designs of local council houses. At the same time Sanderson wallpapers had been chosen for the majority of the thirty houses that were to be built as a result of a competition 'to encourage private enterprise to put forward ideas for a standard, permanent house to be built by private builders'.[12]

Thus the company's exposure in the major post-war exhibitions ran the gamut from the most costly products to the well-designed, less expensive papers for which the firm had also become known; the latter soon included re-released machine-printed flock designs.[13] Other Sanderson offerings included Dersine Fancy Papers, used for box linings and coverings, as wrapping papers, and as product posters, decorative pelmets and side drops for shop displays. Originally instigated in 1935 (when two high-speed crêpe-paper-making machines were purchased), this enterprise was highly profitable, with corporate customers in the 1950s ranging from Lloyds Bank and W. H. Smith to the couture houses of Hartnell and Chanel.[14] This association with fashion houses may have prompted the 'Smart as a Dress from Paris' slogan introduced at the beginning of the 1950s and created in concert with Cecil D. Notley Advertising Ltd, the agency Sanderson used from about 1936 and throughout the 1950s and 1960s.[15]

*The Central Showroom as it will appear in the forthcoming Sanderson exhibition*

By 1950 the Uxbridge factory had been extended to accommodate 120 Jacquard looms alongside those weaving plain cottons, adding high-quality figure-woven textiles to the existing range of printed fabrics. In the following year these new figure-woven textiles were among the Sanderson products exhibited at the Festival of Britain in the *House & Garden* decorative schemes, the West End Restaurant at the Festival Gardens and aboard the *Campania*, the Festival Ship. A heavy silk-flock stripe was used in the Dome of Discovery and Sanderson wallpaper was used exclusively at the Royal Festival Hall.[16]

Despite the generally poor retail sales generated by the 1.5 million visitors to the 'Britain Can Make It' exhibition and the 8.5 million visitors to the Festival of Britain in 1951, along with similarly disappointing sales from the 1950–51 and 1953–54 Arts Council touring exhibitions of contemporary sculpture for the home, which also included Sanderson wallpapers,[17] the company remained committed to re-establishing its brand through such vehicles. There was also the pressing need to inform the public of

what was available. As a result, Sanderson launched a series of its own exhibitions at Berners Street, each timed to coincide with the introduction of new pattern books. These exhibitions were 'Decor 52', for the second set issued after the war, 'Three Arts' for the third set in 1954, and 'Decorama' for the next, in 1956.[18]

While long remembered within the company for its royal visitors (Queen Elizabeth, later the Queen Mother, and Princess Elizabeth, soon to be Queen Elizabeth II) 'Decor 52' was a strategic move to introduce professional decorators (still at this point meaning painters and paper-hangers) to contemporary trends. This was intended to stave off the already apparent competition from amateurs, and complemented the Wallpaper Hanging School that had been initiated at Perivale in 1949. Students, many of them war veterans, were taught basic craft knowledge and new trends. Following on from 'Decor 52', these courses were tailored to learners, improvers or craftsmen.[19]

'Decor 52' was undoubtedly successful, for it prompted the more ambitious 'Three Arts' of 1954. Accompanied by a

No. 45098 (31s. plus 1/8th)

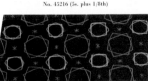

No. 45216 (5s. plus 1/8th)

No. 15191 (6s. plus 1/8th)

No. 15165 (6s. 6d. plus 1/8th)

No. 93456 (8s. plus 1/8th)

No. 54111 (26s. plus 1/8th)

*Left* Inexpensive contemporary wallpapers were machine-produced by Sanderson from 1952; this page from the 'Three Arts' brochure illustrates several, together with hand-printed patterns, with prices given per piece.

*Below left* During the two decades after the Second World War there was a separate studio at Berners Street, which was probably responsible for the design of this hand screen-printed wallpaper of 1954.

*Below right* The Harlequinade Room at Sanderson's 'Three Arts' exhibition, 1954.

*Opposite* H. Stephenson provided this artist's impression of the area in the Sanderson showroom designed by A. J. Milne for the 'Three Arts' exhibition, which opened at Berners Street in January 1954.

*Overleaf* Two fabrics included in the 'Three Arts' exhibition: 'Perpetua' by Lucienne Day (detail, *left*), printed on rayon taffeta in 1952 as a British Celanese–Sanderson joint project, and 'Nautlaus' by the Uxbridge design studio. 'Nautlaus' had been created as part of the Sanderson contribution to the Festival of Britain in 1951.

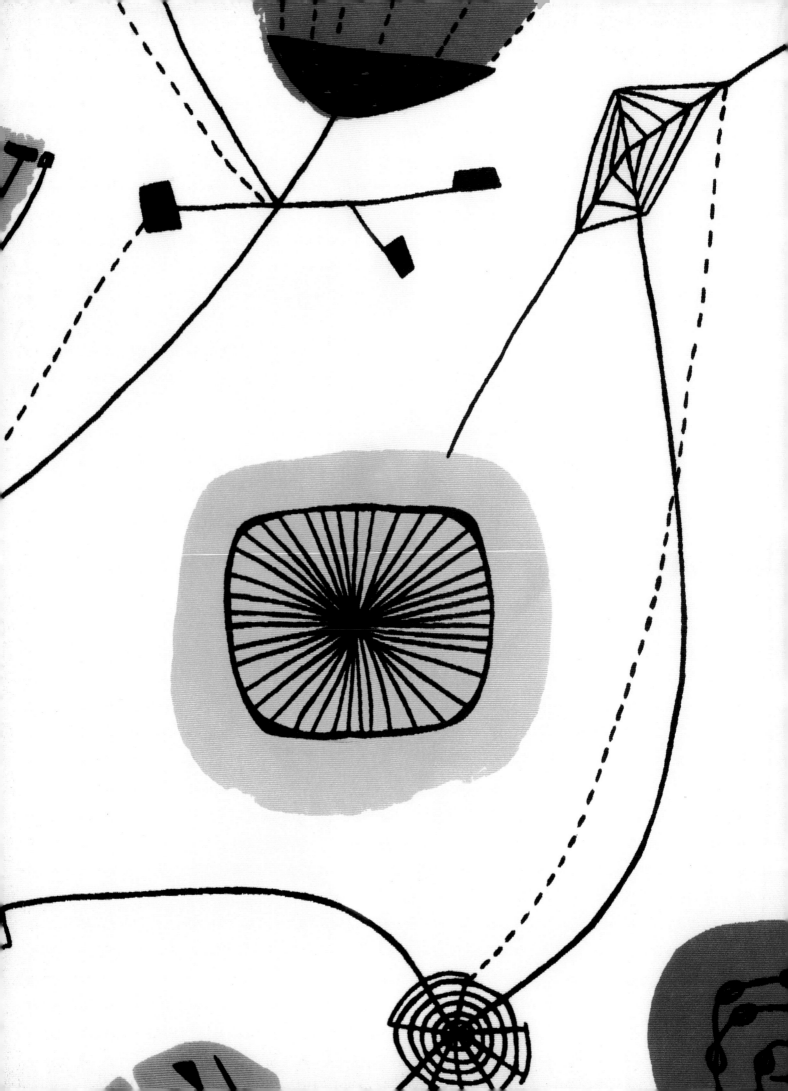

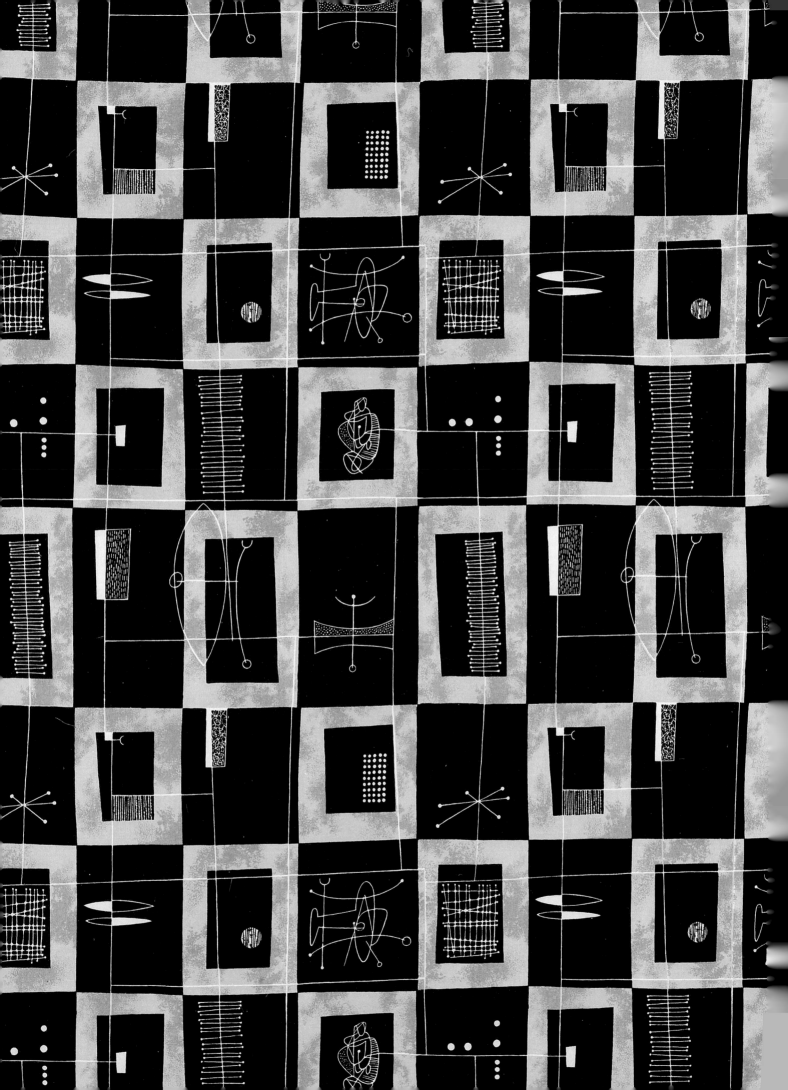

catalogue and advertised as offering 'fresh ideas, new colours and modern designs', it attracted 16,000 visitors in ten days and also garnered extensive press coverage, with features in magazines as diverse as *Ideal Home* and *Design*. The former liked the combination of large patterns with small all-overs, while the latter, the mouthpiece for the CoID, laid stress on the exhibition's 'endorsement of the modern movement in its most recent phase'.[20] Two areas, among them the Harlequinade Room, were designed in-house, while the central showroom was designed by A. J. Milne and included furniture by Heal & Son, Earnest Race and Gordon Russell, rugs by Peter Collingwood, and pottery by Susie Cooper. Among the textiles were three by Lucienne Day: 'Miscellany', 'Perpetua' and 'Climbing Trees', which were among the six Day designs issued in 1952 and 1953 as a British Celanese–Sanderson joint project. Sanderson distributed these fabrics with considerable success, at a time when it 'took courage to commission them' and 'faith and enthusiasm to market them'.[21]

The 1956 'Decorama' decorative schemes were designed by Sir Hugh Casson, working with students from the Royal College of Art (where Casson was professor of interior design from 1955 to 1975) and his associates, including Edward Bawden and Humphrey Spender, whose designs Sanderson also produced for this occasion. Such evident links with the British art and design establishment were very important to manufacturers at the time, having been the focus of 'Painting into Textiles', an *Ambassador* exhibition held late in 1953, when twenty-five artists were paid by the magazine to produce works for translation into textiles. Among these artists was John Piper, who subsequently would play a starring role in Sanderson's centenary celebrations.

A less conspicuous underwriting of talent had already been established through the Harold Sanderson Art in Industry Fund, a trust activated in 1949, which continued to operate for the next

fifteen years. Candidates aged between fifteen and twenty-three were judged on submitted work and each year one received a bursary covering accommodation, attendance at an evening art college and visits to exhibitions and museums while training in the Perivale studio. If successful, the initial six months was extended for up to five years. Thereafter they could choose to leave, many becoming successful freelance designers, or they could elect to stay, as did Paul Haines, who was employed by the firm in 1962, and eventually became Sanderson's wallpaper design manager, first at Perivale and then at Gosport.[22]

For the Uxbridge design studio, both technical and aesthetic changes in the 1950s ensured that there was greater latitude in their approach to developing products. The development of stain-resistant silicone treatments was providing a wider scope in the use of colours 'hitherto found to be unpractical because of their failure to disguise the effects of soiling'.[23] With both weaving and printing facilities to hand, designers could create interesting effects easily, by overprinting a woven pattern, developing co-ordinated weaves and prints, or simply exploring a loom's capacity to produce cloths highlighting the characteristics of unique yarns and textures. This approach was perfectly in tune with contemporary trends, which, by the mid-1950s, expected the designer not only to 'look upon his medium as a painter does his canvas', but to realise 'the inherent potentialities of texture and weave as pattern sources for the material itself'.[24]

Fabrics, as *Design* noted at the time of the 'Three Arts' exhibition, were an increasing part of Sanderson's trade, being supplemented from 1952 by a collaboration with Courtaulds Ltd. The Courtaulds–Sanderson collection, 'Ancestral Fabrics', consisted of twenty-five designs inspired by textiles found in fifteen historic houses in the UK, including Althorp and Hardwick Hall.[25] High demand for woven textiles such as these contributed to the

The Architectural Review November 1957

The emphasis in this
exclusive new Sanderson collection
of hand-prints and screen-prints is on
large-scale designs,
the bolder-stroke colours—
increasingly in demand to-day.

Papers as wide as 28½ inches.
Powerful contrasts; designs based on
brilliant work by Sir Hugh Casson, Walter Hoyle,
Edward Bawden and Bent Karlby.
Exciting papers, equally at home in the
large-roomed house and in hotels, restaurants
and public buildings.

SANDERSON
LARGE HAND-PRINT
CONTEMPORARY BOOK

Arthur Sanderson & Sons Ltd., Berners Street, London, W.1.
AND AT GLASGOW, EDINBURGH, LEEDS, MANCHESTER, BIRMINGHAM, EXETER AND SOUTHAMPTON

*Left* This advertisement for the Sanderson
Large Hand-Print Contemporary Book notes
that wallpapers as wide as 28½ inches (73
centimetres) were available. Issued in 1957,
the book incorporated block- and screen-
printed papers released since 1954.

*Below* Three screen-printed textiles, from left:
an imported Pausa fabric shown in the 'Three
Arts' exhibition, a Sanderson design of 1956 and
a design by Horndean for Sanderson *c.* 1957.

*Opposite* Swedish hand screen-printed linens
by Eric Ewers AB as displayed in the 1954
'Three Arts' exhibition (*left*), together with a
detail (*right*) of two of these linens, which had
been imported by Sanderson since 1951.

eventual need for Sanderson to engage five other weaving firms on its behalf. The collection also inspired the printing of related designs on plain and figured cloths, and on papers. Although much of the British reputation in this period was built on the provision of historic patterns, the contemporary style nevertheless gained ground as the decade progressed.[26]

Sanderson's contemporary offerings were broadened by imported textiles. These were introduced in 1951, and three years later the 'Three Arts' exhibition included a large alcove given over to Swedish printed linens by Eric Ewers AB and elsewhere displayed a black-ground screen-printed cotton undoubtedly by Stig Lindberg, suggesting some Sanderson arrangement with Nordiska Kompaniet, the Stockholm store responsible for Lindberg's printed textiles.[27] Soon afterwards, Sanderson imported Picasso designs produced by Bloomcraft in the United States, followed by prints from Italy, at first from Socota and then from J. S. A. Busto Arsizio. The latter, founded by Luigi Grampa in 1948, printed Gio Ponti's 'I Cirri', the screen-printed cotton that won a Gran Premio at the 1957 Milan Triennale, where Sanderson acquired five designs for their imports range. By 1959 the company was also importing fabrics from the well-known West German firm Pausa. Such arrangements generally operated on the principle of mutual benefit, with Sanderson's distribution expertise providing a bridge for American fabrics into Europe, and European fabrics into the world.

Exports had been a priority for Sanderson since 1946, when the government mandated that one quarter of home-produced textiles and wallpapers had to be exported. In the same year *The Ambassador*, the British textile export magazine, began publication; it was to become the most important record of British textile production for another quarter century, and also covered wallpapers. Sanderson products appeared frequently after 1948, and their inclusion guaranteed wide exposure, for by 1955 the magazine had subscribers in ninety countries. A 1955 feature devoted to 'new textures on the walls' incorporated twelve illustrations, five of them Sanderson wallcoverings, noting that many more papers were now made washable with a coating of matt plastic emulsion (as opposed to glossy).[28] The text highlighted the modernist trend 'to give walls interest of texture and a structural look rather than that of being surfaces merely for superimposed decoration', citing Sanderson's 'Canotex', a 'closely woven jute-canvas treated with a waterproof backing which enables it to be brushed and scrubbed without fear of sagging off the wall'.[29] Another such design was 'Flint Wall', its realism rendered through hand silk-screening, a process Sanderson used at this time to test innovative ideas through its sampling service, sending only the most popular designs on to be engraved. Such products, together with its broad range of prints and weaves, made Sanderson the most successful British textile and wallpaper exporter of this period.[30] This achievement was capped off by

*Right* Sanderson imported five prize-winning fabrics from the 1957 Milan Triennale, including, shown on the right, 'I Cirri', designed by the Italian sculptor Gio Ponti.

*Below right* The design for this machine screen-printed cotton was purchased in 1957 and issued in 1960. Its *trompe l'œil* rendering of folds of cloth was created by Mea Angerer.

*Opposite left* Bloomcraft fabrics imported from the United States by Sanderson include 'Picadors' and 'Carnet' by Pablo Picasso; their selvedges declare not only that they are screen-printed, but also that they are treated with Zepal, a DuPont oil- and water-resistant fluoridising finish available from about 1957.

*Opposite, right* This satin-faced cotton furnishing fabric was flatbed screen-printed by Pausa AG and imported by Sanderson for its 1961 season.

*Overleaf, left* 'Woodcut', a large-scale screen-printed cotton by Cliff Holden, was purchased by Sanderson in 1957 but not issued until early 1963, when Holden won an award from the American Institute of Interior Designers for a WPM Palladio wallpaper.

*Overleaf, right* A mid-1950s wallpaper, hand screen-printed at Perivale for the Berners Street contemporary range.

The Architectural Review March 1958

## INTERNATIONAL PRIZE-WINNERS
## from the XIth Milan Triennale Exhibition

For the first time ever, Sanderson introduce to this country prize-winning printed furnishing fabrics from the great Milan Triennale Exhibition.

New colours take to fabric; striking new ideas unfold. Five tomorrow-minded designs are now presented — five

out of more than four thousand entries submitted in this truly international competition.

This series will be a centre of attention. The fabrics, in altogether seven different colour-ways, can be seen in Sanderson showrooms and are available to order now.

*fabrics exclusive in this country to*

### SANDERSON

BERNERS STREET, LONDON, W.I. AND AT GLASGOW, EDINBURGH, LEEDS, MANCHESTER, BIRMINGHAM, EXETER AND SOUTHAMPTON

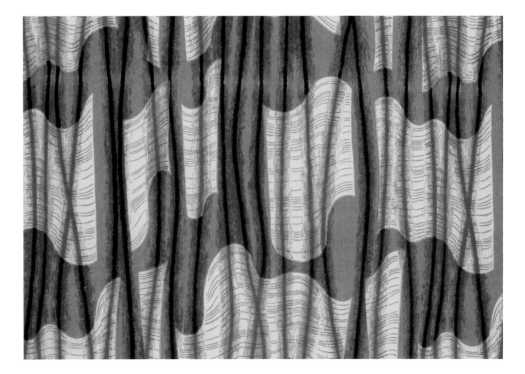

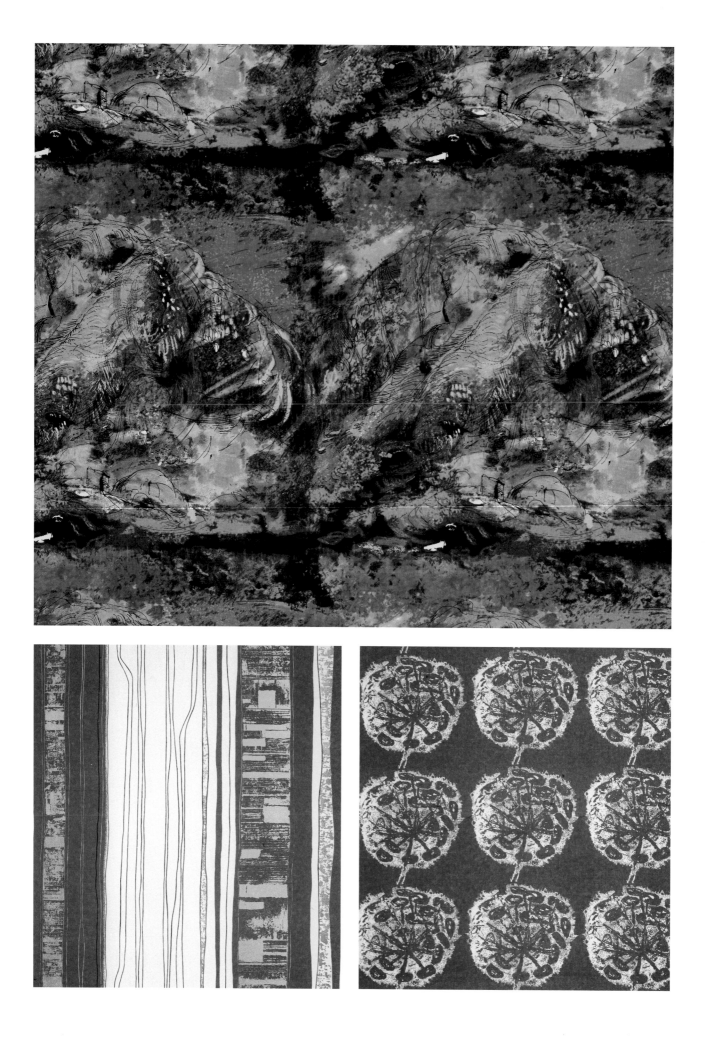

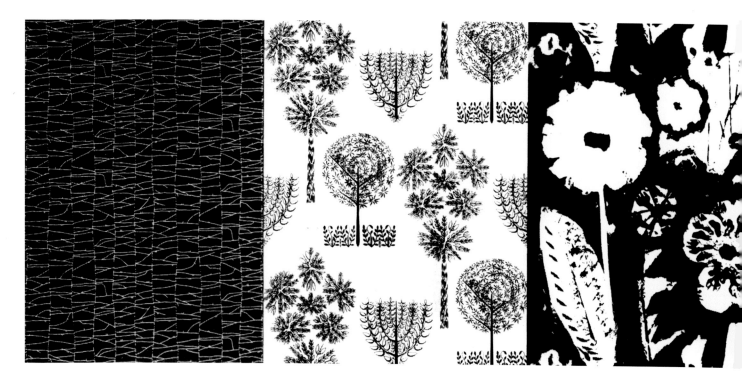

*Opposite, above* 'The Glyders' by John Piper appeared in the 1960 collection, remaining in the range until 1966. It was reprinted for the Piper exhibition held at the Tate Gallery in London in 1983–84.

*Opposite, below left* Jupp Dernbach-Mayen, who designed the mosaic wall in the new showrooms at Berners Street in 1960, also designed this hand screen-printed wallpaper for the Sanderson Centenary Collection.

*Opposite, below right* This screen-printed cotton from the 1960 Centenary Competition Collection was designed by Lisa Grönwell or Maj Nilson, both of whom collaborated with Cliff Holden at Marsland Designers, Gothenburg, Sweden.

*Above* Three patterns from the 1960 Tempora series of contemporary wallpapers, from left to right: 'Runic' by the British designer George Todd, 'Trees' by the American Denst & Soderland and 'Tricus' by the Scottish tapestry artist Gordon Crook, another winner of Sanderson's centenary design competition. Most Tempora patterns were machine printed; 'Trees' and 'Tricus' were exceptions, being hand-screened productions.

*Overleaf* The cover of the booklet produced by Sanderson to celebrate its 100th anniversary in 1960 displays the design by John Piper for the stained-glass window that remains in the Berners Street building to this day.

the firm's receipt of a third Royal Warrant in 1955, from HM Queen Elizabeth II, for wallpapers, paints and fabrics.[31]

In 1957 a long-awaited new building was erected at nos. 58–60 Berners Street, where there had been some war damage. The showroom was by now so well-known for its stimulating displays that 'it became necessary for the firm to ask its decorator customers to refrain from sending their clients…in the afternoons because it was becoming too crowded'.[32] Next door, on the site of the original showrooms, arose 'the world's most fabulous showrooms', which opened in time for the Sanderson centenary celebrations in February 1960.[33] A new showroom was also built at Uxbridge, where collections included fabrics by John Piper, who also designed the two-storey stained-glass window that still remains in the Berners Street building (now the Sanderson Hotel). His design for the window was featured on the cover of *The Ambassador*, which noted in its article about the new building that 'the vast showrooms make tempting and effective areas of selection for the general public'.[34]

The public had already been involved in the Sanderson centenary celebrations through a competition that attracted 3,000 entries from its inception in 1958. Only two amateurs were among the ten winners, who included Peggy Angus, Gordon Crook and Robert Dodd, who later designed many patterns for the firm. A book of hand-printed Centenary Collection wallpapers was produced, containing designs by, among others, Raymond Loewy, Frank Lloyd Wright, Gio Ponti, Fedi Cheti, Jacqueline Groag and Jupp Dernbach-Mayen, who designed the mosaic wall in the courtyard of the new building at Berners Street. Machine-printed papers were represented by the calligraphic 'Tempora' collection.[35] The foreward to the book, by Paul Reilly, director of the CoID, stated that the customer would find 'no retrospection in this series, no wistful regrets of the past'. No statement could have been more apt as the firm looked forward from 1960. Ivan Sanderson became the new WPM chairman at the end of that year, and Sanderson had subsidiaries in Scotland, Australia, Canada, New Zealand and South Africa.[36]

# A New Concept in Co-ordination

- Triad, the ground-breaking co-ordinated Sanderson collection, is launched in 1962.

- In 1962 the majority holdings of John Line and Shand Kydd pass to the WPM.

- Turnbull & Stockdale is acquired by Sanderson in 1965; its Rosebank brand and sales force are absorbed and Rosebank collections continue to be released.

- In 1965 Sanderson becomes part of a newly formed Reed International's Decorative Products Division, together with Crown and Polycell, as a result of their purchase from the WPM by the Reed Paper Group. Spectrum Paint is introduced and Crown and Shand Kydd products are merchanted by Sanderson until 1985.

- Consumers in this period become wealthier, younger and more interested in individualistic styles.

- The 'Young Sanderson' range is introduced in 1968; stretch covers are also introduced in the same year.

- Between 1972 and 1973 the Perivale factory closes and all wallpaper production is moved to Crown wallpaper mills in Gosport and Christchurch; the latter continues to produce Shand Kydd papers under the Sanderson umbrella until both mills close in 1982.

- During July 1975 Sanderson of Berners Street opens as a retail operation in the revamped showroom; the occasion is marked by an exhibition, 'The Decorative Art of the Paper-Stainer', which incorporates examples from the seventeenth to the twentieth centuries, including a reproduction of an eighteenth-century wallpaper shop.

- In 1976 Sanderson acquires a carpet manufacturer, Thomson Shepherd of Dundee.

- The separate wallpaper and fabric design studios and sales force are combined in 1983.

- The company celebrates its 125th anniversary in 1985 with a revamped showroom and an exhibition accompanied by an illustrated catalogue focused on the history of Sanderson and its acquired firms.

For every manufacturer of fabrics and wallpapers, the quarter-century after 1960 was a challenging period of mass reorganisation. It was no different for Sanderson. In 1965 Ivan Sanderson retired as chairman; that same year, the Monopolies Commission forced the WPM to cease functioning as a combine. The WPM shares were purchased by the Reed Paper Group which, as Reed International, was to retain ownership of Sanderson, as well as Crown and Polycell, until 1985.[1] Around the same time, Britain began to use more imported textiles than domestic productions, but Sanderson continued Ivan Sanderson's commitment to technical development and expansion, so strengthening its export marketing that in 1971 the company still dominated overseas sales of British-made fabrics and, especially, wallcoverings.

Despite the announcement in March 1972 that Perivale must close – with the exception of a small hand block-printing unit – the company was able to draw on its understanding of its customers' history to boost domestic sales.[2] Recognising the growing market for direct selling, in mid-1975 Sanderson of Berners Street, as it became known, was redeveloped as a retail operation.[3] Beyond its customary offerings of wallpapers, pastes and textiles, the Sanderson range was expanded to include carpets, lighting and other decorators' sundries such as window blinds and clocks.[4] A prominent feature in the showroom was the 'mixing bar' for Spectrum paints, which Sanderson had introduced in the early Reed years, being the first in the UK to provide this type of flexible colouration.[5] By 1985 even more was on show. From the numerous room-settings, customers could select upholstered sofas, chairs, footstools, dining-room and bedroom furniture, table lamps and rugs, retiring to the coffee shop to consider their purchases or take a break from the surfeit of goods on display.

This wide variety of products was made, from 1973, in the Crown wallpaper factories in Gosport and Somerford, near Christchurch. Gosport had only become a WPM enterprise in 1961; for thirty years it had been run by the Northcott family, who in the end owned some 350 'Brighter Home' shops that distributed their wallpapers. The Christchurch site was the factory of Shand Kydd, which had merged with John Line in 1958. Gravure and flexographic presses were sent from Perivale to Christchurch where vinyl wallcoverings were made, having been introduced at Perivale in 1964. The Christchurch presses were also used to produce transfer-printed fabrics for garments and lingerie, as well as printed paper for laminates, which had emerged out of post-war Perivale experiments in PVC printing. Christchurch also received the new five-colour Stork rotary screen-printing machine (delivered to Perivale in 1971 but never uncrated) together with only fifteen of the old factory's eight hundred employees. At the Gosport factory, flock and gravure presses from Perivale were added alongside the surface-printing machines; some twenty-two Perivale personnel, plus those in charge of Sanderson's international wallpaper business, were

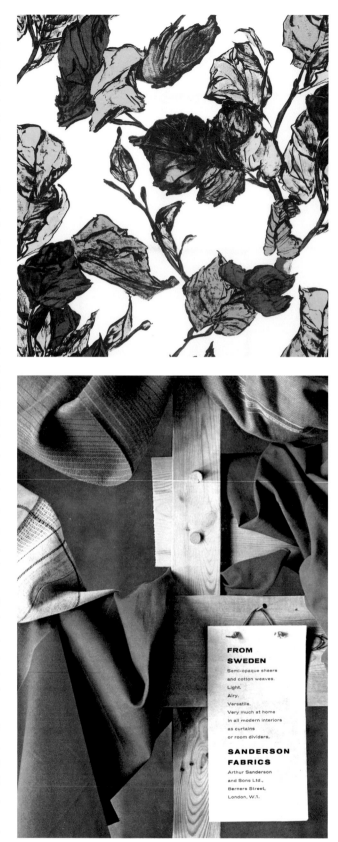

*Previous page and above* In the mid-1960s Sanderson's international offerings included screen prints such as 'Amapola', imported from Pausa AG in 1967 (*previous pages*) and 'Glendale' (*top*), a design purchased from Hans Geller in Germany for the 1964 range. From 1962 semi-opaque woven sheers and cottons with vivid, wide stripes (*above*) were supplied by Swedish firms such as Böras, Ludwig Svensson and Marimekko.

Florals and checks with a modern look.

Screen prints by Sanderson of Berniers Street.

Meet five of the newest arrivals in the range...

also transferred to the factory. Despite these reinforcements, however, the Gosport factory never recovered from the economic impact of the 1972–73 fuel crisis and with the arrival of A. L. ('Lee') Taylor as new chief executive in 1982, both it and Christchurch ceased production.

Having been separate entities up to now – each with its own studio and sales forces – in 1983 fabric production became integrated with wallpaper manufacture, or rather, as Taylor put it, the emphasis of the company changed 'from being a wallpaper company which used a co-ordinated fabric to being a fabric company which uses a wallcovering co-ordinate'.[6] As part of Taylor's reforms, the studios and archive were moved into purpose-built facilities at Uxbridge, where the wallpaper ranges were developed and sent for printing to two Crown mills: Lees of Oldham and Potters of Darwen. Uxbridge fabric printing continued but weaving was now carried out at Dawes of Nelson and BST Silks in Bradford. Both were within much closer proximity to the Crown mills in Bolton, where the former Turnbull & Stockdale making-up services for curtains, covers, bedspreads and cushions had been relocated to a purpose-built site in 1974.[7]

The impetus behind all this development was the need to compete with the upsurge of do-it-yourselfers, who were aided by the WPM's introduction of ready-pasted wallcoverings in 1961. Sanderson itself began manufacturing ready-pasted papers from 1964, using a wet process, and from 1966 via an improved dry process. It also became apparent that a more diverse product range was needed, as the long life of the new vinyl wallpapers (the first of which was ICI's 'Vymura' in 1961) reduced the need for frequent replacement; Sanderson stretch furniture covers and the Young Sanderson range both arrived in 1968. The firm had twelve of its own regional showrooms in this period, but it was also becoming clear that there was growing competition from 'sheds', as the big self-service outlets were known. Over the following decades the 'sheds' would change the market so dramatically that one journalist recently posed the question, 'Does anyone out there remember "decorating shops"?', explaining to younger readers that these were 'modest post-war precursors of B&Q and Homebase, they supplied stock wallpapers, among other things. When faced with an unusually stylish provincial customer, they might give her (it was usually a her) an appointment card for the Sanderson showroom on Berners Street, in the West End of London.'[8] Indeed, by the time Sanderson opened Berners Street as a retail store, it was estimated that 75 per cent of all wallpaper sales were direct to the customer, rather than through a decorator. As a consequence, the Sanderson expansion of its co-ordinated range of products from 1962 onwards turned out to be of paramount importance.

The idea of co-ordination was not new to textiles and wallpapers, but had typically been offered only as a part of the provision of handmade goods, and thus only, really, at the behest

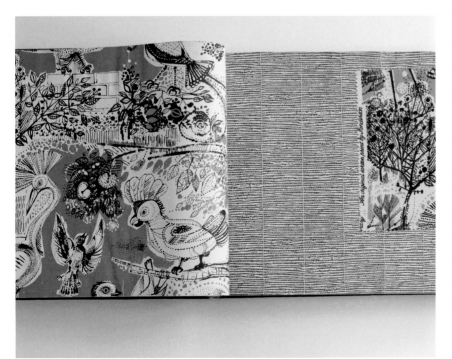

*Above left* Stormur, the brand name for Sanderson fabric-backed vinyl wallcoverings, began production at Perivale early in 1964 with designs such as these, printed on a helio-gravure press.

*Below left and above right* The first Triad collection of 1962 included 'trios' consisting of a matching machine-printed paper and fabric, and a companion paper. Shown here are 'Aviary' (*below left*) and 'Lustre' (*above right*).

*Opposite, above left and below left* Two photographs of the Berners Street premises in the early 1960s. Inside the showroom (*upper image*) projecting panels displayed laminates on the right and wallpapers, including the Tempora range, on the left.

*Page 131 and opposite, right* These striking compositions were created by Notley Advertising Ltd to promote Sanderson's 1964 products in *Architectural Review* and other professional journals. Humphrey Spender, who designed the hand-screened wallpaper (*opposite right*), was then a tutor at the Royal College of Art. Stacked on Eero Saarinen's 'Tulip Chair' (*previous page, fifth from top*) is 'Artichoke', the work of one of his students, Alexander MacIntyre. Third from the top is 'Cantra' by Robert Holmes.

*Overleaf, left* 'Cobweb', a screen-printed cotton, was produced by Calprina for Sanderson's first Triad collection.

# How many young Sandersons can a family run to?

## Young Sanderson wallpapers don't price young people out

Sanderson wallpapers may be used to palaces; but that doesn't mean they're stuck in the last century. Just take a look at the young Sanderson wallpapers. All Sanderson's inborn sense of style is there, but so too is any amount of fresh contemporary thinking—about colours, about patterns, about enchanting your guests. Go and see the young Sanderson wallpapers and fabrics at your Sanderson showroom or stockist—you'll like the prices too. As we said, you don't have to live in a palace to run to lots of young Sandersons.

# Have you seen the young Sandersons?

## 'Utsukushii!' says Our Man

Our Man has a problem. As his mind marvels, his Japanese limps. He murmurs: 'Beautiful!' He is sadly guilty of the understatement of his life. And he knows it!

The decorating jewels that Oda San displays before his discerning eye are some of the new Japanese wall-coverings that anyone in a Sanderson showroom will be just as delighted to display for you. Grass cloths, wood veneers, paper-backed silks, metallic papers. Colours as subtle as a Japanese flower arrangement, as rich as the rising sun. Textures so superbly original that we doubt if even the Japanese have a word for them!

These wall-coverings bring you beauty with the quality of a work of art. Ask Our Man. Having learnt diligently from Oda San, he will tell you that they are, quite simply, the pride of the Eastern World. And before you can stop him, he will repeat it in impeccable Japanese!

### SANDERSON
*WALLPAPERS AND FABRICS*

ARTHUR SANDERSON & SONS LTD. SHOWROOMS: LONDON: BERNERS ST., W.1. GLASGOW: 1-7 NEWTON TERRACE. EDINBURGH: 7 QUEEN ST. LEEDS: 30 LOWER BASINGHALL ST. MANCHESTER: 8 KING ST. LIVERPOOL: RANELAGH ST. BIRMINGHAM: 218 CORPORATION ST. LEICESTER: 81 CHARLES ST. EXETER: HIGH ST. BRISTOL: 4-6 THE HORSEFAIR. SOUTHAMPTON: 65 THE AVENUE. BRIGHTON: 13-29 DYKE RD.

*Previous page* This advertisement for Young Sanderson, a range launched in 1968, appeared in *House & Garden* in March 1969. The black-ground paper was a reissue of 'The Trinidad', designed in *c.* 1900 by the children's book illustrator Miss Bryant.

*Above* In 1967 Sanderson issued this 'Our Man' folding leaflet illustrating room sets and products. Among the textiles are a best-seller by Robert Dodd called 'Ceramica' (no. 2), which had been in production since 1960, and 'Lorenzo' by Robert Holmes (no. 7), which had been issued in 1965.

*Left* Japanese wallcoverings were stocked by Sanderson from 1961 and included highly textured grass cloths as well as more subtly surfaced wood veneers, paper-backed silks and metallic papers. The influence of such costly textural wallcoverings can be seen in the more modestly priced Triad 'plains' on page 133.

Our Man gets his inspiration from the four corners of the world. He goes wherever the really smart designs are and brings them back home for you. Traditional or modern, floral or plain, low-key or colourful—each of his chosen wallpapers and fabrics has that extra touch of distinction that says 'Sanderson'. Follow Our Man's taste through these pages — nine original room sets created especially to illustrate the beauty and diversity of Sanderson papers and fabrics. An exciting decorative combination for every room in your home. See the Sanderson Blue Book at your nearest stockist's—it's the world's finest collection of wallpapers. Also the new Sanderson fabric range. You'll love living with the Sanderson Look!

**SANDERSON**
WALLPAPERS AND FABRICS
Arthur Sanderson & Sons Ltd., Berners Street, London, W.1.
wpm

Wallpaper No. 06605. Fabric No. ZE 955/4 ("Lorna") Cotton; in 5 colourways; 48"/50" wide.

Wallpaper No. 66324. Fabric 1 No. BL 5251/7 Rayon in 25 colourways; 48"/50" wide.

Fabric 2 No. ZH 636/5 ("Parfait") Satin wide.

of the decorator. As in the nineteenth century, 'decorator' in this context meant interior designer, as opposed to the painters and decorators who had formed the Sanderson customer base well into the twentieth century. As early as the 1920s Sanderson had created 'suites' of patterns, in some cases including textiles, through the groupings in its wallpaper books. However, such juxtapositions were intended merely as suggestions for the trade. By the early 1960s it was clear that an appeal needed to be made directly to the public. The result was Triad, a series of keyed-together papers and printed fabrics issued biennially from 1962 until 1980. Its impact was widespread. By incorporating patterns ranging from modern abstracts to traditional floral sprigs, it shifted the definition of 'contemporary' away from design content alone. As Lesley Hoskins has recorded, even the Rasch firm, which was 'so dedicated to modern design in the 1950s that old samples and commercial examples were not allowed in the design studio, complemented its modern ranges with "Country", a coordinated collection including traditional stripes and nineteenth-century rosebuds'.[9] What is more, Triad consolidated Sanderson's consistent promotion of its own pattern books at a time when most books offered to the public were 'collections compiled by merchants from the offer of various manufacturers, generally representing stock carried locally'.[10] The first Triad collection contained sixty-eight trios of two papers and one fabric each, with most of the papers ranging

in price from 10s. to 15s. per roll, the equivalent of about £8 to £12 today.[11]

The promotion of Triad was underpinned by a Notley advertising campaign that built on the Sanderson identity while identifying its products with a wide range of personalities. Initially these were anonymous characters. 'Our Man', a campaign that ran from 1960–63, and was revived in 1965, epitomised the company's sophisticated and eclectic offerings. Early copy claimed 'Our Man' was 'as English as a stately home, as proud of it as Yorkshire is of Yorkshire', going on to declare Sanderson ranges to be 'a home-from-home for the cream of British designers' to be exported all over the world. In return, 'Our Man brings home to England the newest, most original and exciting ideas that the world can offer him.' 'Our Man' starred in the first Sanderson advertisement to feature wallpapers and fabrics together, promoting the first Triad collection; other advertisements showed him returning from his travels laden with goods, lounging in an avant-garde interior, or ruminating over a hand-printed paper. During this time Sanderson introduced a number of Japanese wallcoverings, including hemp and other grass cloths, metallics and paper-backed silks. Fabrics, too, were obtained from overseas firms including Fischbacher in Switzerland and Sigrist in France. As before, designs also continued to be purchased abroad, many from studios in New York; in Paris they were sourced from the studio of Lizzie Derriey

Dessins. In Germany patterns came from the Willy Hermann atelier and from designers such as Leo Wollner, an influential and trend-setting tutor at the Staatlichen Akademie der Bildende Künste in Stuttgart.[12] To drive home the point that the firm's geographically diverse range could appeal to a wide market, advertisements between 1963 and 1965 posed the question, 'What is the Sanderson Look?', accompanied by the catchphrase, 'the luxury look within your reach,' showing a room occupied by an individual, from a baby to a grandmother.

The success of the 'Our Man' and 'Sanderson Look' series – for which the budget was over one million pounds – ensured that the 'inhabited' advertisements continued when the Young Sanderson range was launched in 1968. Intended to convey youthfulness, fun or luxury, this same 'peopled' approach featuring anonymous characters was adopted when the advertising account was transferred to Doyle Dane Bernbach (DDB), whose first series, at the beginning of the 1970s, took the theme 'wallpapers, fabrics and help'. Its amusing realism gave way in 1973 to a corporate campaign of 'Very Sanderson' advertisements showing well-known personalities in their own homes. Among those featured up to 1977 were Kingsley Amis, Joan Bakewell, Petula Clark, Jilly Cooper, Britt Ekland, Peter Hall, Susan Hampshire, Hammond Innes and Diana Rigg.

With the instigation in 1981 of Sanderson's Options range (the replacement for Triad that included bed linen in 1982 and

*Above* Three screen-printed children's fabrics, clockwise from left: 'Pandarama' by Robert Holmes, 1964; 'Puss Puss', a Triad fabric by J. Nash, 1965; and 'Gazebo' by Pat Albeck, 1966.

*Opposite, above* Two advertisements by Notley, who created the 'Our Man' and 'What is the Sanderson Look?' series, the latter shown here in an example from 1963 (*left*). The stretch covers, promoted in *Ideal Home* in March 1969 (*right*), were made possible by vast improvements made to elastic fibres in the mid-1960s.

*Opposite, below* Two advertisements by Doyle Dane Bernbach, one of 1971 promoting Sanderson's Spectrum 75 wallpaper book, which grouped samples into colour ranges (*left*). The other represents the 'Very Sanderson' series, here promoting the 1974–76 Triad range with an image of Petula Clark in her own home in Switzerland (*right*).

*Overleaf* 'Babylon' by Pat Albeck for the 1969 Young Sanderson range, and 'Nagako' by Pat Etheridge, 1973, illustrate the bold colouring and large scale of many Sanderson screen-printed designs issued in this period.

**What is the Sanderson Look?**

**She's terribly, terribly with it!**

She knows about jazz—and she's got her ideas about decoration. She likes having things to show off, so she went for a Sanderson Look that's a talking point with all her friends. Sanderson have something for everyone. Wallpapers. Fabrics. Rich, rare wall-coverings. Colours that blaze, shades that whisper. Treat yourself to the Sanderson Look at eighteen and you'll be doing it all your life. Because only your own experience can prove to you that it takes a pretty good fabric or paper to make the Sanderson grade.

**Wallpapers at Sanderson stockists. Fabrics at all good furnishing retailers. Or see them together at Sanderson Showrooms:** Berners St., W.1, and in Glasgow, Edinburgh, Leeds, Manchester, Liverpool, Birmingham, Leicester, Exeter, Bristol, Southampton, Brighton, Newcastle, Cardiff.

**SANDERSON**

*WALLPAPERS*
*AND FABRICS*

the luxury look
within your reach

**It's amazing what the young Sandersons can do for the family seat**

the first blue-blooded stretch covers

Thoroughly modern young Sanderson stretch covers do more than fit quick. They also live up proudly to a great family name. See the lavish designs they come in. Notice how smooth they feel, how neatly they take the shape of your furniture. They're true Sandersons down to the last zip-fastening.
Can we vouch for these young Sandersons' good

behaviour? So confidently that we give them a year's guarantee. Remember—they're made in double-jersey Bri-nylon with re-inforced seams. You can call them (and you'd be right) the aristocrats of stretch covers; but you don't have to be rich to afford these Sandersons. See the young Sanderson fabrics and wallpapers at your Sanderson showroom or any leading store.

**Have you seen the young Sandersons?**

**By the time you've found your wallpaper will you still feel like decorating?**

Sorting through a motley assortment of patterns is no way to look for wallpaper.
Especially when you know what colour you want.
And have to thumb through all those you don't want.
With this in mind, we've taken a fresh approach to our latest book:

Spectrum 75.
We've grouped all its patterns according to their colour.
Which means you can turn straight to the blues, reds, yellows, or any other colour.
And turn your back on the rest.
Hopefully, this'll save you wasting all your energy at the shops.

When you could be putting it to better use at home.

**Sanderson**

Wallpapers, Fabrics and Help.

**Very Petula Clark, very Sanderson.**

Photographed in Miss Clark's chalet in the

**Sanderson**

Wallcovering: FG3076. Curtains and patterned cushions: ZH364/2, striped cushions: AF530/4, all 100% cotton.
Settee fabric: BL5850/30, 100% cotton with acrylic finish. All from the new Triad Collection.

today still offers a more complex array of co-ordinated products) came the change in agency to Butler Dennis Garland. By 1984, however, Sanderson was back with DDB and the 'Very Sanderson' series, this time featuring Liza Goddard and Michael and Mary Parkinson. The 'Very Sanderson' concept secured such a strong response for the company that it was used thereafter until 1990 for the entire range: traditional woven fabrics, William Morris coordinates, and even the simplest of wallcoverings and cloths were styled 'Very Plain, Very Sanderson'. Only in overseas markets was the 'Very Sanderson' concept understood to be expecting too much of the average consumer, who for a decade from the mid-1970s was instead tempted by the phrase, 'You don't have to be English to appreciate Sanderson'.

Alongside Triad and, later, Options, Sanderson continued to offer other collections. In 1965 the Rosebank collections came under the Sanderson umbrella, offering fresh floral prints styled by George Lowe (who became design director upon the amalgamation of all Sanderson studios), and woven fabrics styled by Peter Smith.[13] In 1966 Sanderson had taken over the production of Palladio wallpapers, originally a WPM line conceived in 1956 by Richard Busby, director of the Lightbown Aspinall branch. These sets of large-scale screen-printed papers were intended for use by architects in large public spaces, and were issued approximately every two years. Palladio 7, the first of these to be printed at Perivale, was followed in 1968 by Palladio 8, which included

the first screen-printed vinyls produced within the WPM. The twenty-two designers commissioned for this collection produced papers with stylised florals, bold Deco geometrics and pop-art patterns, some using metallic colours. Among those contributing were Pat Albeck, Inge Cordson, Robert Dodd, Deryk Healey, Zandra Rhodes, Jeremy Talbot and Eddie Pond, then the director of the WPM studio. Dodd, of course, was already well known to Sanderson, and Albeck was to contribute some of the most characteristic patterns of the era. Her fabric designs for 1969 and 1970 were featured in *The Ambassador*, with 'Babylon', for the 1969 Young Sanderson range being described as 'spectacular'.[14] Bold, large-scale patterns such as these – especially those inspired by inter-war Art Deco motifs – were especially fashionable by 1970 but can be found in the earlier and influential Sanderson Odeon collection. Designed by Pat Etheridge and Robert Holmes for the 1967 season, Odeon consisted of six prints and four woven fabrics related through style and colour (and thus also presaging the Options concept). One fabric design by Holmes, 'Bye Bye Blackbird', was still receiving attention from *The Ambassador* in late 1970, at a time when this magazine maintained its great influence abroad.[15] In 1971 came a similarly striking collection in Palladio 9, the first Palladio collection to be sold overseas; according to Pond, it created 'unprecedented demand'.[16]

The bold graphic style continued to set the pace into the mid-1970s whether the pattern itself was traditional, a contemporary

*Right* These large-scale screen prints, 'Aspasia', by Pauline Green (left), and 'Pashonata' by Charles Raymond (right), were issued on a heavy cotton-satin rep in 1964 and 1965, respectively.

*Opposite, above* All screen-printed fabrics, Robert Dodd's 'Silurian' (in the background, far left) was a cotton satin; the other fabrics in the background (from left to right): 'Carfax' by John Wright, and 'Alpha' and 'Omega' by Tony Sharp – were cotton–linen blends. These sold in 1965–66 for about 23s. a yard, half the price of the imported linen in the foreground, designed by Paul Bonheim, which retailed for 45s. a yard.

*Opposite, below* Two DDB advertisements for Triad ranges show the shift from bold Op interiors in 1970, here dressed in 'Mineret' (*right*), to those with countryfied charm, evident in a 1976 room decorated with 'Kalao', attributed to Brian Elesgood (*left*).

**Sanderson Triad.**
Wallpapers and Fabrics that go together.

The Sanderson Room
Where sensational things start to happen

Let your imagination go. Picture what
Sanderson Triad could do for your rooms.
    Sanderson wallpapers, Sanderson fabrics,
combined with Sanderson flair. That's the Triad
collection. A three-way transformation. Where
a ravishing fabric echoes a wallpaper and
contrasts a rich but plain wallpaper.
    Then consider the Sanderson Young Set
and Palladio wallpaper collections.
    But see them first. At wallpaper shops. And
in better department stores everywhere.
    And come away with some sensational ideas.

# Sanderson

floral or, increasingly, taking its inspiration from the Art Nouveau era. As the decade progressed, 1970s designers looked further backwards from the inter-war years to the turn of the century, before settling upon the period from 1870–90. This gave Morris patterns – which had been produced by Sanderson fairly consistently since 1927 – renewed popularity. The inclusion of 'Blackthorn' in the 1976 Triad collection can be pinpointed as the watershed moment when Victoriana became the rage. 'Blackthorn' was also produced in a reduced-scale version, called 'Blackthorn Minor', indicative of the trend towards smaller patterns, which was increasingly evident by the late 1970s. Actually designed by John Henry Dearle in 1892, this Morris & Co. pattern remains in the range today, having not only inspired a dozen imitations during the 1970s, but also becoming an international ambassador of the Sanderson brand as it became increasingly well-established around the world. The global appetite for the English country-house style cannot, of course, be credited to Sanderson alone, but there is little doubt that the company's ability to hand-print Morris patterns and its continual provision of chintzes gave it a particular caché in this regard.

The Sanderson archive played its part in other ways too, providing the source material for an exhibition of three centuries of papers, friezes and decorations for walls, which marked the 1975 opening of Berners Street as a retail enterprise. Similarly, it enabled the firm to mark its 125th anniversary with another

exhibition at Berners Street, entitled 'Sanderson 1860–1985'. By this time Sanderson was restabilising itself after two decades of significant changes, and was entering another period of expansion, much of it buoyed up by the rage for chintzes. This quintessentially English style is so much a part of the Sanderson story that the following chapter is devoted to it alone.

*Above* 'Blackthorn', designed by John Henry Dearle in 1892 for Morris & Co., was promoted in the 1976 Triad book with this litho. It became part of the Options ranges for about a decade beginning in 1981, and at that time had a companion Sunway Matchmates blind.

*Opposite* Originally a Jeffrey & Co. block-printed wallpaper designed *c.* 1900 by Walter Crane, 'Cornfield' was adapted by Sanderson designer Pat Smart and reissued in the 1984 Options 2 collection as both a surface-printed wallpaper and the rotary screen-printed cotton shown here.

*Overleaf* 'Lost Summer' was purchased from the Parisian design studio Lizzie Derriey Dessins in May 1973, and approved for production in the general range in November 1974. By 1977 it was also being printed for Habakuk in South Africa. Its enlarged stylised flowers, inspired by Art Deco florals, are a motif typical of the 1970s.

# 'Whole Hoggers' on Chintz

¶ In 1984, at the peak of the fashion for the English country-house style, Sanderson opens its own decorators' showroom in New York City.

¶ WestPoint Pepperell, Inc. of Georgia purchases Sanderson from Reed International in 1985.

¶ Carpet manufacturing is moved to new premises in Bolton in 1986, operating there for another dozen years, the last two as Thompson Shepherd Carpets, following a management buyout.

¶ Sanderson acquires the John Watson wallpaper mill in Lower Darwen in 1987, moving all of its wallpaper production to this site, including the hand block-printing, which was transferred to the Anstey Wallpaper Co. during late 2003 and early 2004.

¶ In 1989 WestPoint Pepperell is aggressively acquired by Farley Industries; in the following year Sanderson is sold to the largest textile manufacturer in the Netherlands, Gamma Holdings NV.

¶ Berners Street is closed in 1992 and a new Sanderson showroom and shop opens at 112–120 Brompton Road in London's Knightsbridge area. In 2001 it relocates to the King's Road.

¶ In the early 1990s the company establishes the Sanderson Gallery, a collection of home accessories, gifts, decorative products, travel goods, china and toys, which are manufactured at the Sanderson making-up workshops in Bolton or by outside contract suppliers.

¶ Uxbridge ceases manufacture at the end of December 1999.

¶ In August 2000 Sanderson's new headquarters are established in Denham; seven months later, in March 2001, there is a management buyout.

¶ In August 2003 Sanderson goes into receivership; three weeks later it is purchased by Walker Greenbank plc.

n 1908 the *Journal of Decorative Art* declared that 'Fashionable London is "whole hoggers" on the chintz and kindred styles this year, and the style is sure to spread to the Provinces.'[1] By 'chintz' was meant a particular type of wallpaper, rather than cloth, although features shared by both at this time were realistically rendered flowers, whether in posies or on undulating vines, and a glazed or varnished surface. While some patterns might err towards the exotic, as appropriate to the Indian colonial origins of the style, or incorporate birds, striped grounds, or a lightly sketched background pattern, the beauty of the drawing itself remained paramount. Although other firms produced chintz papers, the three Sanderson brothers set an early benchmark for quality, according to the *JDA*. 'The big developments in their business took place in the early [eighteen] eighties, when amongst their other designs, they brought out a series of floral papers with the distinctive touch of the English brush. They took the public taste with a rush; they possessed all the daring of colour of the French designs, with a breadth and quality entirely their own. The pre-eminence which they then established they have never since lost in this particular line.'[2] The point, it seems, was that there was 'a world of difference between the Sanderson Chintz and the ordinary production; and while a well-printed and designed chintz makes a charming decoration, the indifferent chintz is a truly appalling affair.'[3] A century after such designs made their appearance in the Sanderson range, and over sixty years after they were offered on cloth as well, a series of advertisements issued between 1978 and 1980 under the catchphrase 'our roses are so much the richer' stressed, among the firm's other unique aspects, its ability to machine-print cloth in twenty colours. As one insider put it, 'at the peak of its success the technological gap between Sanderson and its rivals was incredible'.[4] As had been the case in the previous century, the complex chintz designs popular in the 1970s and 1980s provided ideal showcases for the firm's superior technical abilities.

The advertisements' point about Sanderson's skill in machine-printing was no small matter, for it was in this arena that Harold Sanderson had first achieved so much at Chiswick, 'whence was to come in the early [eighteen] eighties the papers that finally gave the quietus to the primacy of block-printed goods'.[5] Although block-printed chintzes were produced – and the acquisition of Woollams in 1900 extended the Sanderson range of these sorts of papers – it was the provision of the less-expensive machine-printed chintz wallcoverings that permitted the style to gain so much momentum. Chintz was favoured by the fashion for neo-Georgian interiors in the homes of the wealthy from about 1890, which in simplified form remained a popular middle-class style well into the 1970s, when the more softly worn splendour of the English country-house style began to be very gradually reincarnated.

The term 'chintz' itself first appeared as a descriptive term for wallpapers around 1900, confirming this as the moment when the style had established widespread recognition. Demand was such that by May 1912 a Sanderson sales representative, Mr Pike, was urging the board to make up a 'Chintz Book' for the year 1913. Initially the directors were of the opinion that chintzes were adequately represented in their various pattern books, but by November they had reconsidered, making a few books for Berners Street alone. In April of 1913 they relented further: 'it was resolved to make up 300 books for the year 1914 containing machine papers from -/6d to 3/-, 200 for Mr Jameson, plus 50 each for Mr Horne and Mr Pike'.[6] At the same time the directors were discussing the introduction of fabric printing, which would include more than one pattern in the chintz style, and it is significant that these fabrics were to be called 'cretonnes' to avoid confusion with the by then well-established chintz papers.

Although there is some ebb and flow in the background treatments and colourations of chintzes over time, it is difficult to date particular patterns without reference to records such as those found in the Sanderson archive. One example of this phenomena is a surface-printed neo-Georgian paper which, at the beginning of the twentieth century, was printed with a black-and-white tabouret-stripe ground. Thirty years later it was also printed with a more subdued manilla and cream stripe, and in that form it was used as the cover and endpapers for the first trade edition of Cecil Beaton's *Scrapbook*, published by Batsford in 1937.[7] When Beaton designed the striking black-and-white costumes for the Ascot racing scene in the 1964 film *My Fair Lady*, his accurate evocation of the Edwardian period – down to his incorporation of black-and-white tabouret-striped ribbons – revitalised the taste for Edwardian chintzes presented as they first were, with crisply-delineated hues, and one could be forgiven for dating the circa 1905 paper to the 1960s. Such cyclical variation in background and colouring is also common among the lush,

*Previous page* An Edwardian surface machine-printed paper, probably adapted in the Sanderson Chiswick studio from a Woollams pattern.

*Opposite, above* This advertisement, one of a series by Doyle Dane Bernbach (DDB) for Sanderson, 1979, features 'Aimée', designed by Robert Holmes, heir apparent to Kenneth Truman. A classic 48-inch Sanderson floral, it was introduced in 1979, subsequently adapted to 54-inch linen union and satin and remained in the collection until 1997.

*Opposite, below* Detail of a Woollams wallpaper, hand block-printed to a design registered in January 1852. Sanderson machine-printed the same design in 1979 under the name 'Magnolia', and included it in the Sanderson Chintz Wallpaper collection launched in August of the same year.

# To save pennies, some manufacturers prune their roses.

On the right is a piece of fabric printed the way most manufacturers would print it.

In only eight simple colours.

On the left, a piece of Sanderson fabric called Aimée.

It's printed in no fewer than twenty colours.

Clearly, ours is the more expensive process.

But then, just as clearly, our roses are so much the richer.

## Sanderson 🌟

ARTHUR SANDERSON & SONS LTD., BERNERS STREET, LONDON W1A

*Above* This machine-printed neo-Georgian style
paper was issued by Sanderson *c.*1905 and,
recoloured in warm tones, was still available
in the 1930s.

*Opposite* 'The Queen Anne Chintz' was designed
for Jeffrey & Co. *c.* 1909 by one Turner, probably
the landscape artist William Larkin Turner. Its
subsequent surface-printing by Sanderson,
which began in 1929 and continued until 1973,
accounts for the pencilled grid and notes.

more florid chintzes. These have had a remarkably good run, with an exceptional example being 'Rose and Peony', first launched as a wallpaper in 1914. It was redesigned as a printed fabric in 1929 and released the following year, and by the 1960s it had been produced in twenty-eight colourways to suit changing tastes. With the addition of a matching wallpaper, it was issued in the 1972 and 1978 Triad collections. The pattern is still produced on both paper and fabric today, the latter on linen union as well as on cotton.

Given their longevity as patterns, the right colouring is essential to make a particular chintz timely. The combination of warm oranges and greens seen in a surface-printed cretonne designed by Eric Haward in about 1927 characterises that period, as does its closely ranged tones, in this case fifteen of them. (The printing of up to twenty colours on *paper* had been achieved at Chiswick three years earlier, and Sanderson was at the time capable of printing in up to eighteen different colours on fabric.) In contrast, cooler harmonies were the hallmark of

patterns produced from the latter part of the 1930s until about 1950. The importance of colour in the decoration of an interior – often the deciding factor – led Sanderson to arrange some of its trade pattern books by colour, rather than pattern, as early as 1931. Equally, it informed the development of the range of paints, which since about 1966, under the single Sanderson brand, Spectrum, has offered at least 1,350 colours in four finishes: vinyl matt, silk emulsion, eggshell and gloss.[8] The base recipe allows for an infinite number of colours, since any shade falling between the named colours can also be produced. During the 1980s, as the fashion for floral patterns was in full sway, advertisements showing arrangements of many-tinted blooms promoted the paints' ability to match every colour occurring in nature.

It is easy to assume that the chintz style was consistently in demand, but this is not quite the case: there have been periods when designs were modified to make them either more 'authentic' or less noticeable. From the mid-1920s well into the 1950s, for example, background tones were far less often white, a detail

*Left* In June 1926 Eric Haward was paid just over £22 for the design of this Eton Rural Fabric, which was surface machine-printed a year or so later and remained available until 1947.

*Opposite* Sanderson lead-free Spectrum paints, introduced in the mid-1960s, were advertised in 1989 with a hand-tinted photograph by Charles Settrington, reflecting the then-global fashion for floral patterns.

of some importance, since the use of a mid-toned ground eliminated any strong contrasts and rendered the pattern less conspicuous, as well as giving it an air of some age. On the other hand, dark grounds, which have appeared about every third or fourth decade since the 1910s, create a decidedly contemporary impression. The swing from white – the most authentic background – to faded to dark can be prompted by any number of variables. In the mid-1930s it was the craze for the exotic that reactivated interest in white-ground chintzes for walls. Commenting in 1936 on the Sanderson stand at Olympia, one reviewer praised a room decorated in an authentic Chinese Chippendale pattern, probably inspired by a recent Chinese exhibition at the Royal Academy of Arts in London,[9] and went on to note that 'the Chintz pattern (which, after all, has Chinese relatives) is attracting attention'. The Sanderson scheme in question employed a white-ground 'quilted' chintz in panels, leading the reviewer to suppose that chintz papers might reappear as 'enlivening notes'.[10] By late 1937, modernism was deemed 'somewhat hackneyed' and a review of Sanderson's 1938 set declared 'Perivale believes in the chintz revival. It is not a general revival, but it seems to be a real one. Probably two kinds of customer encourage it; those who knew the old chintzes and revert to them after a course of the abstract, and those younger ones to whom they come (also after much abstract pattern) as a delightful novelty. The simple fact is that chintz, following a convention of

venerable age, has great value as pattern, and will never suffer permanent eclipse.'[11]

As the chintz revival in the late 1930s indicates, the placement of a particular pattern in an interior can be paramount to its success. On the 1936 Olympia stand, the Sanderson chintz had been displayed for a bedroom; such patterns were typically confined to bedrooms in this period. Deeply embedded cultural memories have ensured a continued use of chintz patterns in boudoirs and bedrooms for several centuries. In the eighteenth century the introduction of chintzes from India into Britain was often in the form of bed hangings. Folding screens, once requisite for stylish bedrooms and boudoirs, became dressed in chintz papers for similar reasons, and screens with Sanderson papers were supplied in America by W. H. S. Lloyd in the first third of the twentieth century).[12] Sanderson's floral fabrics had been made into eiderdown bed covers more than a half-century before the firm added bed linens to its ranges in 1982.

External events such as exhibitions could transform a traditional pattern into a thing of the moment. For post-war chintzes, this was the case in 1960, when the Victoria and Albert Museum mounted an exhibition entitled 'English Chintz', an enlarged version of a show that the museum had orchestrated for the Cotton Board's Colour Design and Style Centre in Manchester five years earlier, which had enabled British designers and fabric producers 'to appreciate more clearly those special qualities of

photography by charles settrington

# Spectrum Paint

1350 colours for interiors, in four finishes, vinyl matt or silk emulsion,
eggshell and gloss – 1044 for exteriors.

# Very Sanderson
Berners Street, London, W.1.

*Above* The striking 'Sweet Bay' wallpaper and glazed cotton were designed by Alison Gee of the Sanderson studio and released in September 2007. A dark, expansive, lacquer-like ground also conveyed modernity in chintzes produced around 1910 and 1940, and became popular again in the mid-1980s.

*Opposite* This advertisement, promoting the fast colours of Sanderson fabrics in 1950, depicts one of the first fabrics issued after the lifting of wartime rationing in 1949. Its pastel ground is typical of many mid-century chintzes.

sun-resisting

and washproof

Bright and refreshing—
now and for years ahead,
because Indecolor fabrics
will not fade in use or
"run" in the wash.

SANDERSON
INDECOLOR        FABRICS
and have you seen the new ideas in        SANDERSON WALLPAPERS?

Is it
curtains
for
Sanderson?

fine drawing [and] craftsmanship, which people overseas have long associated with British furnishing fabrics.' In its coverage of the 1960 exhibition, under the banner 'The New Chintz Tradition', *The Ambassador* went on to predict that the show would 'stimulate and revitalise the whole field of furnishing textiles and interior design' and 'that the wealth of our design tradition becomes an inexhaustible point of departure for every kind of design from the most literal to the most abstract interpretation'.[13] William Morris fabrics were included in both exhibitions, for by the 1960s 'chintz' meant simply 'printed textile'. In truth, the chintz style allowed for a three-dimensionality that was antithetical to Morris, who believed that pattern should exist in a flat plane with, at most, a secondary plane behind to suggest density and natural growth.[14] Nevertheless, the intermingling of both types of floral patterns had the three-fold effect predicted by *The Ambassador*. It opened the way for new florals, provoked global interest in Morris patterns and traditional English chintzes and contributed to the establishment of a more broadly defined chintz style, which is now as inextricably linked to England as are tea and marmalade, despite their similarly foreign origins.

The mixture of Morris patterns and traditional chintz styles is typified by the work of Kenneth Truman, who joined the Sanderson studio in 1939, at the age of thirty-five. He arrived at a time of awakened interest in Morris patterns, which had suf-

fered a decline in popularity since the 1920s. Just a year before Truman took up his brush for Sanderson, the *JDA* reported that the 'school of thought on contemporary design which is represented by the Design and Industries Association and similar bodies has been giving attention to wallpaper and – a little surprisingly in some ways – has come down, not only on the side of pattern, but of floral form based on the teaching of William Morris. The resulting patterns are in no sense "cribs" of the work of Morris, but they are unmistakably in the Morris tradition.'[15] Often producing several designs each week until he retired in 1969, and then working part-time until his death in 1977, Truman's forté was his ability to work quickly in a manner that

*Opposite* Highlighting the Sanderson curtain-making service launched in 1965, this Notley advertisement of 1968 features 'Ischia', issued in 1965 and produced in the range until 1978.

*Below left* 'Latymer', commissioned by Michael Parry and designed by Glenda Kilshaw in 1989, is advertised here in an English country-house setting. The 'Very Sanderson' concept, developed by DDB in 1973, was used until 1990.

*Below right* Bed linen, added to the Sanderson range in 1982, often featured traditional floral patterns. 'Janine', based on a mid-nineteenth century document and designed in-house by Janine Rose (who later became Sanderson's design manager) appeared in this 1991 advertisement aimed at the international market.

JANINE IN FINE COTTON PERCALE

Latymer

Very Sanderson

Berners Street, London, W.1.

Sanderson

LONDON · PARIS · NEW YORK

Berners Street, London, W1. Telephone: 071-636 7800.

*Above* Showing the flower-painting skills of Paul Haines, at work in the Perivale studio, this image was used in an 'Our Man' advertisement in 1962 that was released in both English- and German-language versions.

*Below left* Among Kenneth Truman's many
floral designs for Sanderson was 'Ifield', a
31-inch sixteen-colour machine-printed linen
union offered from 1966 until 1968.

*Below right* The Options collection of 1994,
which introduced wallpaper borders and printed
voiles, was promoted via contemporary
photography, at the time considered a dramatic
move away from the traditional interior shot.

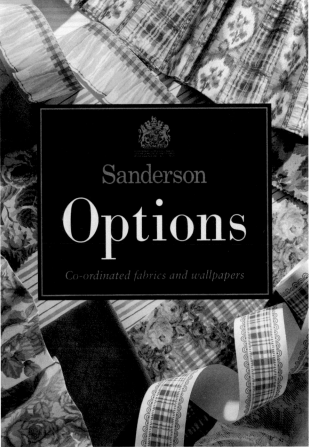

combined all the élan of a traditional chintz with a measure of
simplification in the flowers that gave his designs a contemporary
touch. In 1984, not long after the company's annual turnover
reached £23 million (something like £60 million today), it was
held that 'the Sanderson reputation for English floral designs is
based almost entirely on [Truman's] output'.[16] The success of
Truman chintzes, which have since appeared in subsequent
Sanderson ranges, engendered an optimistic mood in 1984, the
year of Sanderson's 125th anniversary.

By its anniversary year the business employed close to one
thousand people (albeit approximately half the number
employed in 1972), ranging from hand-printers to young designers such as Gillian Farr (who was soon to be design manager and
would stay with the company until 1996),[17] and interior-design
consultants based at Berners Street, who for £25 would produce
a presentation board based on a visit to the customer's home.
Sanderson had begun to link its name with interior decoration in
other ways, too. The last Triad collection was launched in 1980

with a series of rooms designed by an international selection of
decorators, including Lilo Horstadius of Sweden, Jean-Paul
Person of the French magazine *Maison et Jardin*, Gian Luigi
Pieruzzi of Italy, Christl Röhl of Germany, the New York-based
partnership of Lucretia Robertson and Donna Lang, and Olive
Sullivan, then decoration editor for *House & Garden* in the UK.
Within four years Sanderson had expanded its North American
business, opening its own interior decorators' showroom in New
York and securing representation in other showrooms across
America. However, domestic retail opportunities were not neg-
lected. A new retail shop opened in Dublin in 1983, and the
company embarked on a Sanderson Specialist scheme to 'concentrate Sanderson's resources into outlets capable of offering
required standards and service levels appropriate to the
product.'[18] In return for measuring, fitting, cut-and-sew services
and paint-mixing capabilities for wallcovering and paint specialists, each retailer received training and advertising support as
well as subsidised pattern books, samples and display units.

# HOUSE
# & GARDEN

INCORPORATING WINE & FOOD MAGAZINE

**Extensions**

**One-room living
on the grand scale**

**Storage solutions**

**Floor treatments -
carpets to stencils**

When Sanderson was sold to the American firm WestPoint Pepperell, Inc. in 1985, and then, via holding company Farley, Inc., to the Dutch firm Gamma Holdings, this concept, although modified, remained the basis for further expansion.

By the mid-1980s the Sanderson brand was closely associated with the English country-house style, but diversity within the range was being encouraged in several ways. The Rosebank brand was reactivated for fresh florals. In addition, after Sanderson had begun printing sheeting for WestPoint Pepperell's expansion into Europe, two contemporary ranges of vinyl wallcoverings and fabrics, designed by Sanderson in 1986 and 1988, were released under the Martex name, a WestPoint brand already well-known in America.[19] In about 1991 a wide range of accessories was introduced under the banner of the Sanderson Gallery, which included items covered with contemporary patterns as well as with the popular chintzes. Aside from the accessories, in the UK alone Sanderson's range of its own and licensed or subcontracted products was extensive, comprising fabrics, wallcoverings (among them miniatures for doll's houses), ready-made and made-to-measure curtains, upholstered furniture, bed linen, paint, brushes, varnishes and wallpaper strippers. These were offered through over two thousand independent retailers; many were also available through concession 'stores within stores' at Army & Navy, Bentalls, Binns, Debenhams, Dickins & Jones, Dingles, Fenwicks, Harrods, House of Fraser, Jollys, Kendals, Leekes, Rackhams and Selfridges.

But this was a difficult time for every supplier of home furnishings. The recessions of the 1970s and early 1990s took their toll, as did stylistic trends towards minimalism and the fad for loft living, which favoured the use of untreated and industrial materials for decorating. Wallpaper manufacturers were particularly hard hit: across Europe and America their numbers were reduced by 50 to 60 per cent in the two decades up to 1995 and thereafter sales worldwide continued to decline.[20] Under WestPoint Pepperell, Sanderson – captained by Lee Taylor –

*Opposite, left* Even at the height of the chintz craze, Sanderson, true to its heritage, continued to issue modern designs. Among these were the Martex fabrics and vinyl wallcoverings depicted in this 1988 advertisement by Charles Settrington, the noted British photographer who became Earl of March and Kinrara in the following year.

*Opposite, right* 'Tea and Sanderson' was the catchphrase used in this 1985 advertisement developed by Judith Woodfin, the first CEO of Sanderson USA, and illustrated by Paul Davis. The slogan encapsulated the firm's international reputation for English country-house style.

*Overleaf* A softer, 'aged' and eclectic interpretation of vintage patterns typifies the recent historic decorative style. Shown here is the screen-printed linen 'Pavia', inspired by a document of *c.* 1880, together with two colourways of 'Beaufort', adapted from early seventeenth-century embroidery designs. Both were part of the Country Linens collection, launched early in 2008. The Spectrum paint colour is 'Russet Lime'.

consolidated its wallpaper and carpet manufacturing, relocating the factories to Bolton and Lower Darwen in Lancashire, and weathered the storm throughout the 1990s, when the order office continued to receive 3,500–4,000 telephone calls each week, despite the downturn.[21] The company was stretched: it had to service its own manufacturing, extensive licensing, retailers in the UK and exports of 40 per cent of its products to over seventy countries. The exports included Sanderson's French distribution, which it had controlled since 1988, and liaison with its own subsidiaries in Canada and the United States.

During the last years of the 1990s, BST Silks in Bradford, Sanderson Carpets in Bolton, and Dawes in Nelson were sold. Printing ceased at the Uxbridge site as the new millennium dawned, few new collections were issued thereafter and the company went into receivership in 2003. Three weeks later the entire business was offered for purchase by sealed bid. Competition for the sale was considerable, a testament to the power of the 'extraordinary world-renowned heritage embodied in the Sanderson and Morris & Co. brand names, the wonderful Sanderson archive [and] strong international licensing partnerships' that to a large degree had been built on the global appetite for chintz of all sorts.[22] Alberto Riva, sole distributor for all Sanderson products in Italy since 1998, has no doubts about the nature and popularity of the 'Sanderson look': 'In several international markets, like Italy, this look is still based on the traditional English country style.'[23] This is particularly the case in Japan, where Price & Pierce had the Sanderson agency from about 1966 and, in the reorganisation of 1982, Nishikawa Sangyo Co. Ltd licensed the Sanderson brand, as it still does today.

# Moving with the Times

§ In 1997 Sanderson has rapidly growing markets in Eastern Europe and the Pacific Rim, where it deals directly with retailers in Malaysia and Indonesia and operates licensing arrangements in Japan, Taiwan and Australia.

§ The Studio Sanderson collection of contemporary fabrics and wallpapers is launched in 1997, followed by three others, one consisting solely of woven fabrics, between 2000 and 2002.

§ A company quality policy is adopted in 1999, promising to provide 'outstanding service which ensures that good design is easily accessible to the Customer'.[1]

§ Following its acquisition by Walker Greenbank plc in 2003, the Sanderson bedding license is sold to Bedeck Ltd and the making-up division is closed.

§ In 2004 Walker Greenbank invests heavily in product development and almost two years' worth of collections are launched in the second half of that year, culminating in the return of new Options collections in January 2005.

§ The Sanderson showroom relocates to Chelsea Harbour in 2005.

§ Revenues increase by 25 per cent in 2007–8.

§ In March 2010 Sanderson celebrates its 150th anniversary with a special collection of fabrics and wallpapers inspired by its archive, a three month-long exhibition at the Fashion and Textile Museum, London, and this book.

§ Sanderson is the oldest surviving English brand name in its field.

However important it has become for Sanderson, chintz was never the entire story. In 1997 it was noted that Sanderson 'is recognised globally for classic and timeless printed florals, but also for an increasingly contemporary offering of weaves as well as prints with an appeal for the younger consumer'.[2] Its ranges that year included a bed linen styled in-house from a Woollams's chintz paper of 1847, as well the first of four Studio Sanderson collections, called 'Earth and Air', conceived by Jaine McCormack (design director from 1997 to 2001) and including designs by Alison Gee.[3] At the same time, however, the firm was supplying papers, carpeting and paints for staff and guest accommodation at Windsor Castle, and within the previous decade had also supplied papers, damasks and other woven fabrics for Balmoral, Buckingham Palace, St James's Palace and Sandringham, many of these in formal, historic styles that were quite different from either the chintzes or contemporary patterns. The company still produced many 'plains', whether textured wallpapers that would have made Harold Sanderson proud, or weaves with simple colour and yarn-effects.

All this diversity might lead one to wonder how to describe the real Sanderson identity, but it can be easily encapsulated in one word: organic. From the very beginning, when Arthur Sanderson moved from importing French goods to manufacturing his own, through the years when his sons transformed machine-printed wallpapers into objects of esteem and used their production capacity to make box papers, wrapping papers and – under his grandson – laminates, one can observe a constant advancement, an ability to move with the times. And like all exemplars of vigorous growth, there are times when pruning is essential if new blooms are to appear.

That the 'pruning' was hard is in little doubt. It was clinically orchestrated by John McLean, who in 1998 had been appointed by Gamma Holdings NV to carry out a review of their UK interests, including Sanderson, where McLean became managing director from early 2000 until August 2003.[4] Current members of staff who were employed in the 1980s are unanimous in marking the closure of Uxbridge as the most significant change for the company. As one employee who joined in 1989 remembers, the Uxbridge site 'was fantastic, we had a bowling green, bar, large staff canteen, tennis courts, football pitch, cricket pitch and pavilion and fishing lake. We had a great social club with lots of activities…trips to Antwerp, theatre trips, barbecues, inter-office games, discos, etc.'[5] Another, who has worked at Sanderson since 1983, notes the reduced staff levels now, but stresses that 'the one thing I will always remember is the friendliness of the people over the years; it is one of the reasons us "old-timers" are still here.'[6] This sense of community is still felt even by former members of staff, as sales director David Walker, who has been with the firm since 1987, notes: 'I often come into contact with ex-employees who always recall their time at Sanderson with great affection and retain a real loyalty to the company.'

Aside from the many staff who lost employment, the cessation of Uxbridge printing had an impact further afield. Its highly skilled hands and high-quality machinery had for some years served outside firms such as Collier Campbell, Osborne & Little and Marks & Spencer, the latter putting its own name to Sanderson-designed patterns and, like the others, also placing substantial orders with the wallpaper factory in Lower Darwen, which continued to operate until 2004.[7]

Although no one carrying the Sanderson name remains with the company, it still retains something of the character of a family firm through the long-standing connections of its staff. Italian distributor Alberto Riva, who began his career in 1964 as a Sanderson representative, succeeding his father, says that his most vivid childhood memory is of a presentation of a Sanderson wallcovering collection in Rome in 1954, when he was ten: 'I was in Rome with my father as a gift-trip at the end of primary school and I remember being very impressed by a product in relief called flock which had a tremendous success with the audience.'[8] In Denham there is another employee who

*Previous page* 'Pompom', a gravure-printed wallpaper designed by Maggie Levien and released in March 2007.

*Above and opposite* 'Spirit' (*above*) and 'Heath' (*opposite*), the latter designed by Alison Gee. Both patterns appeared in the first Studio Sanderson collection (conceived by Jaine McCormack in 1997), and were re-released in the Fresh Florals collection in January 2004.

*Overleaf* 'Mereville', designed in the Sanderson studio for September 2008, is a silk and viscose embroidery (*left*) inspired by an eighteenth-century Spitalfields silk. 'Mereville' cushion and curtains are shown accompanied by 'Brianza' velvet upholstery and 'Elyan' and 'Trianon' embroidered cushions (*right*).

is part of a Sanderson dynasty: Clare Deville, whose father joined the company as a rinse-tank minder in 1948, at the age of fourteen, staying for almost forty years, latterly as production manager in the Uxbridge factory. Her mother joined at the age of nineteen as a colour-matching clerk in 1963, and the two married in 1965.[9] Clare herself has been the manager of customer services since 1999, carrying on Sanderson's long-established reputation for the personal touch as her team of twenty answer some 2,000 calls each week, respond to emails and website enquiries and monitor suggestions from customers.

Walker Greenbank has not been blind to the importance of such continuity. Immediately following its acquisition of Sanderson in August 2003, Michael Parry, Sanderson's former commercial director who had worked for the company for thirty years, was asked to return from retirement to serve as managing director, charged with stabilising the business and reinvigorating the product development plan.[10] Parry brought to this role his experience in developing Sanderson's first bed linen collection, creating its first Options collection and later redeveloping the Morris & Co. range, expanding international licensing and working with the royal households. As commercial director he had been responsible for UK and export sales, the Sanderson archive, the design studio and the merchandise and marketing departments. In late 2004 Parry moved to a consultant's role and David Smallridge, previously managing director of Harlequin Fabrics & Wallcoverings, became managing director for all of the Walker Greenbank brands, the remainder of which

are Harlequin, Zoffany and Morris & Co. While it is still managed by Sanderson, the continued separation of the Morris & Co. brand – a change dating back to 1990 – indicates the present faith in the Sanderson name alone. Together these two brands have amply rewarded their parent company. Revenues grew by 25 per cent in 2007–8, led by woven fabrics, followed by wallpapers.[11] This success was not achieved without facing two challenging years following the acquisition by Walker Greenbank. During this period Sanderson retail concessions were sold to Bedeck, together with the bedding licenses that supported them, and the made-up products division was closed.

In return, however, one could say that Sanderson returned, if not quite to 'the bosom of its family', at least to its milieu. Walker Greenbank's strategic decision to concentrate on the wallpaper and fabric elements of Sanderson's business was backed by the corporation's ownership of the largest surviving manufacturer of quality wallcoverings in the UK, Anstey Wallpaper Co. On paper, non-woven, vinyl and specialist paper substrates, Anstey offers the rare combination of surface-, rotary-, flexo-, gravure-, long-table flat-screen and hand block-printing, the last utilising the 342 printable sets of blocks that have been preserved by Sanderson.[12] In addition, Walker Greenbank owns one of the country's few top-end fabric-printing companies, Standfast & Barracks. By 2005 nearly all Sanderson printing was undertaken by these two factories, restoring the direct links between production and designing that had for so long informed the Sanderson style. Walker Greenbank

*Above left* A selection from the Sanderson Spectrum paint range, which was relaunched in late 2004.

*Left* Sanderson tableware has been produced by Churchill China in Stoke-on-Trent since June 2007. Shown here is the 'Sweet Bay' bone-china dinner service, a pattern taken from the fabric and wallpaper designed by Alison Gee and based on nineteenth-century botanical illustrations in the Sanderson archive.

*Opposite* Michael Parry, David Smallridge and Alberto Riva, who between them have close to ninety years of experience at Sanderson, are seated on chairs upholstered with, from left: 'Copacabana' by Alison Gee, 'Dandelion Clocks' by Fiona Howard (both from the Options 10 collection) and 'Woodland Ferns' by Alison Gee, all 2009.

*Overleaf, left* The Sanderson studio created 'Oakwood' from a lino print for the Options 10 collection, launched in January 2009. Since its inception, Options has been relaunched every three years and continues to maintain its strength in the marketplace.

*Overleaf, right* This predominantly linen fabric, 'Lilia', was introduced in March 2007 as part of the Pompom collection of prints and wallpapers, designed by Maggie Levien and offering a fresh perspective on the post-millennium fashion for Eastern styles.

has also rebuilt the Sanderson design team. The in-house studio is now led by design director Liz Cann, design manager Rebecca Craig and designers Alison Gee, Claire Hart and Helen Sydney, who can also call on three consultant designers – Helen Carey, Maggie Levien and Linda Robinson – or commission work from freelance designers such as Maggie Farmer and Philip Jacobs.[13]

Links with other English manufacturers are also in place. Some Sanderson weaves are made in Darwen at Herbert Parkinson, part of the John Lewis Partnership, and at Abraham Moons, a woollen mill in Leeds.[14] Sanderson's ceramic tableware collections, which were introduced in about 1995, continue to be updated and are now made by Churchill China plc in Stoke-on-Trent. Sanderson paints, too, are made under licence in the UK, by Bradite Ltd, which is based in Wales and continues to use the original Spectrum formula. The Sanderson website, meanwhile, indicates the continued global presence of the company, listing forty-eight other countries, from Mexico to Malaysia, where the firm's British-made products can be purchased.

True to its heritage, Sanderson has under Walker Greenbank looked for other ways, besides printing, to provide the luxury look that has been a lynchpin for the company since its founding. Damasks and similar woven fabrics have been part of the ranges since 1931, and sheers since at least the 1970s, but to these have been added rich velvets and embroideries manufactured for the company in Europe and India, respectively. In their three-

*Above left* For the Autumn 2007 range, Alison Gee developed 'Etchings and Roses', inspired by the engraved prints she consulted at the Musée de l'Impression sur Etoffes in Mulhouse, France. The design was produced both on a glazed linen-union fabric and as a gravure-printed wallpaper with metallic highlights.

*Left* Sanderson bed linen includes Jacquard-woven designs such as the 'Antonia' ensemble, designed and produced by Bedeck (Sanderson's bed linen licencee).

*Opposite* The September 2008 Marney collection, a suite of small-scale wallpapers and cotton and linen prints, was styled by Linda Robinson from eighteenth-century French documents.

*Overleaf* 'Oriental Poppy' (*left*) and 'Persian Poppy' (*right*), both Jacquard-woven in a viscose and polyester blend, were launched in August 2007. The design concept originated with Juliet Hawkins, an in-house Sanderson designer at the time; 'Persian Poppy' was commissioned from freelance designer Andrew Whitworth.

dimensional contours these velvets and embroideries hark back to the leathers, flocks and 'plastic prints' that can be found in the Sanderson archive.

The archive provides not only the 'roots' that continue to sustain new growth, but also the 'DNA' that defines the company's direction. It contains designs and end-products by Sanderson, the eight companies summarised in Chapter 3 and others, including Rottmann & Co. and Birge, as well as 'documents', meaning textiles and wallpapers unrelated to the company's trading partners or acquired firms.[15] It also holds company records, production logs and other documentation, along with a design library started by Arthur Sanderson and extended by Harold Sanderson. Examples of nearly every Sanderson fabric produced in the last eighty years are preserved, an initiative begun by John James Nightingale, the Uxbridge factory manager from 1921–24, and continued from 1925 by Ivan Sanderson and Barton Thomas, who was head designer throughout the 1930s. There are an estimated 12,000 Sanderson wallcoverings alone (about 10 per cent of its output), among the many other papers, making the archive one of the three major wallpaper collections in Britain, alongside those of the Whitworth Art Gallery and the Victoria and Albert Museum. The company began donating items to the latter in Harold Sanderson's time, not only papers, but also objects initially purchased for design inspiration, such as a Chinese screen.[16]

*Above* Designed in the Sanderson studio from a document in the company archive, 'Velutti Stripe' has been in the range since September 2007.

*Opposite* 'Sunflower', a large-scale pattern designed in 1960 by Pat Albeck for the Lightbown Aspinall Palladio Magnus 2 collection of architectural wallpapers, was reissued in the 150th Anniversary collection in March 2010.

*Overleaf* 'Dandelion Clocks', by freelance designer Fiona Howard, was created as a printed fabric and wallpaper and interpreted as an embroidery for the 2009 Options 10 collection.

The diversity within the Sanderson archive inspires innovation as much as any particular style associated with the company. Its vast holdings are consulted by outside licensees and makers of non-branded products, and well as by Sanderson's own designers. The vitality and optimism that went into the old wallpapers and cloths still seeps from the archive's drawers and boxes, engendering a verve that is captured in the present collections and felt keenly by the current managing director: 'With 150 years now completed the future looks very bright indeed for Sanderson. Exciting new product and marketing initiatives are set to continue the story of recent growth and there is every reason to expect that the business will still be a world leader in interior furnishings as it celebrates its 200th anniversary in 2060.'[17]

# Royal Sanderson

- Early in the twentieth century Sanderson wallpapers are submitted to the Royal Household for consideration.

- At the Ideal Home Exhibition in 1922, Princess Mary visits the Sanderson stand and selects a wallpaper for her bedroom.

- In 1923 Queen Mary selects a triple-flocked wallpaper for the Blue Drawing Room at Buckingham Palace.

- In 1924 Arthur Bengough Sanderson becomes holder of the Royal Warrant as Purveyor of Wallpapers and Paints to HM King George V. This is said to be the first Warrant granted for the supply of these products.

- The Duke of York visits Sanderson's Chiswick factory in 1924, and the new Perivale factory in 1930.

- Several young men employed by Sanderson attend the annual Duke of York's Camp, which existed from 1921 until 1939 and was enjoyed both by public schoolboys and those from industrial areas or occupations.

- Sanderson's second Royal Warrant is granted in 1951, as purveyors of wallpapers and paints to HM King George VI. The Warrant probably arose from the production of a hand-printed double-flocked paper ordered earlier that year as an exact replacement of the Pugin design hung in the Robing Room of the House of Lords.

- 'Decor 52', an exhibition held at Berners Street, is visited by Queen Elizabeth (later the Queen Mother), Queen Mary the Queen Mother, and Princess Elizabeth, soon to be Queen Elizabeth II.

- In 1955 Ivan Couper Sanderson becomes holder of a third Royal Warrant, this time from HM Queen Elizabeth II, for wallpapers, paints and fabrics.

- In 1964 Princess Marina visits the Sanderson stand at the Ideal Home Exhibition.

- In 1970 the replacement Pugin design hung in the House of Lords in 1951 is produced again for the Royal Gallery and the Queen's private robing room. The original block-printer is later brought out of retirement to print another seventy-six rolls for two committee rooms in the House of Lords.

- During the Jubilee year of 1977, the Berners Street showroom is visited by Queen Elizabeth the Queen Mother.

- Throughout the 1980s and 1990s Sanderson continuously supplies the royal residences with decorative items including wallpapers, paints, damasks and printed and woven fabrics.

- Following a fire at Windsor Castle on 20 November 1992, and the subsequent restoration programme begun in June 1994, throughout 1997 Sanderson supplies papers, carpeting and paints for staff and guest accommodation.

- In anticipation of Sanderson's 150th anniversary in 2010, Queen Elizabeth II sends 'warm, good wishes to all those involved with the company during this most special anniversary year'.

- Sanderson continues to supply goods to the Royal Household, having retained a Royal Warrant for some eighty-six years.

*Opposite* Painted by Richard Jack, RA in 1927, *The Blue Drawing Room* depicts the drawing room in Buckingham Palace hung with a Sanderson wallpaper selected by Queen Mary in 1923. This was the first time the room had been papered, having previously been hung with silk.

*Overleaf* An early 1920s surface-printed wallpaper incorporating a metallic pigment.

*Page 185* 'Magnolia Embroidery', by Alison Gee for the September 2007 Parchment Flowers collection. The pattern was produced both as a gravure-printed wallpaper (shown here) and as a viscose embroidery on linen ground.

# Acknowledgments, Picture Credits, Notes, Further Reading and Index

I would like to express my gratitude to those who have contributed to the making of this book: Debra Barker, Katina Bill, Duncan Burton, Anna Buruma, Patrick Clancy, Alan Cook, Susan Crewe, Clare Deville, Linda Eaton, Jenny Ellery, Phoebe Fox-Bekerman, Julie Gardiner, Cath Haddock, Rozanne Hawksley, Zoë Hendon, Elisabet Hidemark, Bernard Jacqué, Melissa Kennedy, Sue Kerry, Judy Lindsey, Isobel McKenzie-Price, David Nicholls, John Ould, Kelly Parnell, Grace Right, Alberto Riva, Zandra Rhodes, Kevan Rosendale, Celia Rufey, Ruth Shrigley, David Smallridge, Philip Sykas, Edward Turnbull, Paul Turnbull, Mary Turvil, Alan Todd and David Walker, and for the use of their notes and research, previous archivists Caroline Aram, Eleanor Gawne, Lesley Hoskins, and Christine Woods. In the management of this project at Sanderson, special thanks go to: Jo Eaton, Creative Projects Co-ordinator, Labaika Ashiru, Graphic Design Manager, Sarah Addy, Graphic Designer, Liz Cann, Design Director, Rebecca Craig, Design Manager, Alison Gee, Senior Designer, Claire Hart, Designer, and Selina Carbutt, Executive Assistant – who, always helpful, oversaw the flow of information, access to the Sanderson archive and orchestration of the majority of the photography. Victoria Blair, Marketing Director at Sanderson, instigated and orchestrated many celebratory projects to mark the 2010 anniversary, including this book, and assisted in the selection of product images for the final chapter. I would particularly like to acknowledge the contribution made by Sanderson's consultant and former Managing Director, Michael Parry, who was generous with both his time and his extensive knowledge. Finally, I could not have hoped for a better editorial, design and production team at Thames & Hudson, and to all there I express my admiration and thanks.

Mary Schoeser

## PICTURE CREDITS

For a list of abbreviations, please see Further Reading.

## Chapter 1: *The Business Begins*

1. 'A Visit to Messrs. Arthur Sanderson & Sons', *JDA*, September 1890, p. 132.

2. Correspondence between Sanderson and Zuber & Cie survives from 1872 and is held in the archive of the Musée du papier peint, Rixheim; this information courtesy of Bernard Jacqué.

3. Danois received a gold medal at the Paris Exposition Universelle in 1878 for 'imitations de tapisseries anciennes et articles riche', and ceased production in 1894, when his work continued under Alfred Hans (see also note 6); see Véronique de la Houghe, *Art and artistes du papier peint en France: Repertoire alphabetique* (Paris: Gourcuff Grade nigo, 2007), pp. 60–61. I am indebted to M. Jacqué for pointing out this entry.

4. Others state that Balin's association with Saegers only began in 1867: see Teynac, p. 141; Nylander, pp. 246–47; Oman, p. 278; Hoskins, p. 182.

5. Bernard Jacqué in Hoskins, p. 181.

6. Ibid., p. 181. In 1877 Balin began legal action against several competitors who had imitated his designs. When he committed suicide in 1898 after decades of financial trouble, the Alfred Hans factory took control of his business.

7. 'A Visit to Messrs. Arthur Sanderson & Sons', *JDA*, September 1890, p. 132.

8. Cowtan wallpaper order book, March 1864–December 1866, vol. 10, July 1866, now in the Department of Designs, Prints and Drawings, Victoria and Albert Museum 96.A.11, E.1872–1946 (NRA 29140 V & A Mus.). The order was for Mrs Bliss of Beaumont Street, Oxford, perhaps the wife of the then late Dr Bliss, latterly known for assisting Sir Frederic Madden towards his appointment as Keeper of the Department of Manuscripts at the British Museum.

9. He would also have been aware of the impact of the Cobden–Chevalier Treaty, which was signed in January 1860 but only gradually came into force. It probably accounted for the elimination of taxes on British-made wallpapers; the charges had been reduced in 1847 and were abolished altogether in 1861, making wallpapers manufactured in England more affordable.

10. Joanna Banham in Hoskins, pp. 145–48, citing *The Builder*, 25 (1867), p. 362.

11. Greysmith, p. 156, citing *Papers concerning the history and manufacture of wallpaper, and the firm of Jeffrey & Co., 1876–1925*, National Art Library, London MSL/1971/185–189, MSL/1971/198.

12. *Hints on Household Taste in Furniture, Upholstery and Other Details* (London: Longmans, Green and Co., 1868). Eastlake trained as an architect but never practised in this field; his views on decoration were widely adopted by other writers and the 1986 reprint of his 1878 edition is still available today. The content of his book was drawn from articles that first appeared in the London journal *The Queen* in 1865.

13. *Trade Marks Journal*, 20 June 1894, p. 523.

14. Sugden, p. 139.

15. 'Art and Wallpapers', *Commerce*, 10 April 1901, p. 701.

## Chapter 2: *'Of Exceptional Quality and Taste'*

1. Christine Woods in Hoskins, p. 152. The trend towards merchanting increased as the end of the century approached.

2. Sanderson was born 13 April 1829 and died 11 March 1882; his obituary appeared in *The Times* on 17 March 1882.

3. 'A Visit to Messrs. Arthur Sanderson & Sons', *JDA*, September 1890, p. 132.

4. Ibid., pp. 135–36.

5. Woods, p. 13.

6. Elizabeth Aslin, *The Aesthetic Movement: Prelude to Art Nouveau* (London: Elek Books, 1969), p. 79.

7. For further information on the development of this product, see Woods in Hoskins, p. 154.

8. 'Paperhangings Pattern Books for 1888', *Supplement to The Journal of Decorative Art*, March 1888, p. xvi.

9. Quote from an unpublished history of the firm written between 1921 and 1928, incorporated by Bill Sandford into a longer typescript history of Sanderson's factory at Perivale, written 13 June 1978, p. 2.

10. 'A Visit to Messrs. Arthur Sanderson & Sons', *JDA*, September 1890, p. 135. The firm also sold basewad paper, a compressed paper used in the base of the shell, which was probably the paper 'board' used by decorators when cleaning stencils.

11. Ibid. The introduction of these picture-rod mouldings appears to have been something for which the company became well known, since it was remarked in 1907 that mouldings had been sold by Sanderson 'from the beginning'; see 'Messrs. Arthur Sanderson's New Showrooms 54 & 55 Berners Street, London, W.', *JDA*, July 1907, p. 245.

12. 'Paperhangings Pattern Books for 1888', *Supplement to The Journal of Decorative Art*, March 1888, p. xvi.

13. In 2007 these prices were equivalent to £4 for the 12-yard machine-print and £160–400 for the Japanese papers.

14. 'Trade Changes Etc', *The Furniture Gazette*, vol. 14, July–December 1880, p. 144. Corbière had premises at 30 Cannon Street and 88 Queen Victoria Street; upon his retirement their stock was transferred to one Mr. Ernest Miroy of 71 Queen Victoria Street. Corbière entrusted the remainder of his business to Mr G. H. Chapman, another employee of long standing.

15. Moncure D. Conway, *Travels in South Kensington: With notes on decorative art and architecture in England* (New York: Harper & Brothers, 1882) p. 103.

16. Founded in 1837, when it was known as the Government School of Design, it became the National Art Training School in 1853 when it moved to South Kensington, with the Female School of Art in separate buildings; it was also informally called the National Art Schools. In 1896 it was renamed the Royal College of Art.

17. Oman, catalogue nos. 777 (Brooks) and 1031 (Kingman); both papers were given to the museum by Corbière in 1868, together with another paper (no. 1152) designed by an F. A. Slocombe; if the artist was Frederick Albert Slocombe, he would have been about twenty years old when his design was produced.

18. 'Paper Hangings, 1887', *JDA*, April 1887, p. 62, where the popularisation of dado, filling and frieze schemes is said to have resulted from Charles L. Eastlake's 1868 publication *Hints on Household Taste*.

## Chapter 3: *The Milieu*

1. The Carlisle & Clegg branch existed in Derby until 1928, when it was accommodated in new premises built for Lightbown Aspinall; it continued to produce its own sets of pattern books until 1939. A Carlisle & Clegg pattern book is one of thirteen in the collection of Manchester City Galleries that were given to the museum by the Wallpaper Manufacturers' Association in 1933.

2. 'Messrs. Wm. Woollam and Co.', *JDA*, September 1890, p. 172.

3. 'Art and Wallpapers', *Commerce*, 10 April 1901, p. 704.

4. See John Moyr Smith, *Ornamental Interiors: Ancient and modern* (London: Crosby Lockwood, 1887), pp. 60–62.

5. Quoted in Woods, pp. 25–26.

6. Aubert was possibly a descendent of Didier Aubert, a Parisian paper-stainer who had been an employee of Jean Michel Papillon in the 1730s.

7. For a useful summary of Morris's wallpapers see the Victoria and Albert Museum's online resources at http://www.vam.ac.uk/

collections/prints_books/features/Wallpaper/William_Morris/index.html

8. Joanna Banham, *A Decorative Art: 19th century wallpapers in the Whitworth Art Gallery* (Manchester: Whitworth Art Gallery, 1985), p. 66.

9. See Christine Woods, *The Magic Influence of Mr Kydd: Blocked and stencilled wallpapers 1900–1925* (Manchester: Whitworth Art Gallery, 1989), pp. 4–6.

10. I am grateful to Duncan Burton for shedding light on the complexities of merchanting and production at Shand Kydd during this period.

11. See Schoeser in Hoskins, pp. 234 and 238.

12. Woods, p. 26; to which much of this entry is indebted; see also p. 21 for Stahl, who had come to Sanderson from America.

## Chapter 4: *To Serve the Decorator*

1. 'Paper-Hangings in 1902', *JDA*, January 1902, p. 16.

2. 'Paperhangings for 1891', *JDA*, May 1891, p. 79.

3. 'Wall Coverings', *The Artist*, June 1898, pp. 84–85.

4. Distemper itself could only be used on walls that were dry, removed from reach and in a clean environment, a factor that made wallpapers an important element in the arsenal of painters and decorators. See Walter Pearce, *Painting and Decorating* (London: C. Griffin & Co. Ltd, 1907) pp. 97, 143–44 and 261.

5. 'Art and Wallpapers', *Commerce*, 10 April 1901, pp. 695 and 700. In addition to the London sales force, 'travellers' were retained to serve decorators outside the city.

6. Recent photographs by Geoffrey Rippingdale of the Voysey building, as well as of the Sanderson 1893 factory, can be seen at http://www.pbase.com/gripp/chiswickw4.

7. Woods, p. 5, referring to *Sanderson Minute Book 1900–1915*, 5 November 1902, p. 22; the number of books excluded those containing ceiling papers and relief patterns, which had yet to be finalised. The current value uses the retail price index.

8. 'Paper-Hangings in the New Century', *JDA*, January 1901, p. 28.

9. 'The Wall-Paper News: A Review of the Season's Patterns, 1903', *JDA*, January 1903, p. 28.

10. Hahr's designs were published in *Meddelanden från Svenska Slöjdföreningen* (The Journal of the Swedish Society of Industrial Design), vol. 1, 1898, p. 130; she was one of the first Swedish artists to have patterns printed in Sweden, crediting her own name; these were produced by the Kåberg firm, which had previously insisted that all of its patterns had to come from Germany or France. This information by courtesy of Elisabet Hidemark.

11. For Rigby see 'Mr George R. Rigby, Uttoxeter', *JDA*, June 1904, pp. 168–72. Other designers noted are John Cantrill and Miss Bryant.

12. David Edgerton, *The Shock of the Old: Technology and global history since 1900* (London: Profile Books, 2006), p. 69.

13. 'Wallpaper Manufacturers, Ltd: Sanderson & Son Branch', *JDA* (special supplement), September 1905, p. 16.

14. 'Paper-Hangings in the New Century', *JDA*, January 1901, p. 28.

15. 'Our Duty Towards Wall Papers', *The Artist*, June 1898, pp. 86–87; the block-printed transparent (or watercolour) tints were described as 'somewhat "sloppy" work'.

16. 'The Wall-Paper News: A Review of the Season's Patterns, 1904', *JDA*, March 1904, p. 86. Fab-Ri-Ko-Na was a trademark; the phrase 'permanent shades' was used in Wiggin's Son's advertisements.

17. See Katherine S. Howe, Alice C. Frelinghuysen and Catherine H. Voorsanger, *Herter Brothers: Furniture and interiors for a gilded age* (New York: Harry N. Abrams, 1994).

18. Herter Brothers records, Winterthur Library, Joseph Downs Collection of Manuscripts and Printed Ephemera, col. 93, box 14, 1 and 6 December 1904. In 1937 this frieze was still recalled as 'possibly the most successful sporting subject ever featured in a wallpaper' ('Decorators' Exhibition at Brighton: Some Attractive Exhibits', *JDA*, October 1937, p. 339).

19. 'Charming English Friezes', *The Craftsman*, vol. 8, part 1, p. 123.

20. See, for example, 'The Wall-paper News: A. Sanderson & Sons Ltd, 52 Berners St. W.', *JDA*, March 1905, p. 99.

## Chapter 5: *The 'Mecca of Paperdom'*

1. Quoted in Woods, p. 15.

2. 'The Wall-paper News: Arthur Sanderson & Sons Ltd, 52 Berners Street, London, W.', *JDA*, January 1914, p. 31.

3. 'Messers. Arthur Sanderson's New Showrooms 54 & 55 Berners Street, London, W.', *JDA*, July 1907, p. 245.

4. 'Sanderson's Wall-paper Display Stand' *JDA*, April 1909, p. 141, where it is illustrated; a set of six stands cost 15*s*.

5. 'Arthur Sanderson and Sons, Ltd', *JDA*, May 1913, p. 194; on the Gilmour doors' introduction, the *JDA* ('The XIII Annual Exhibition, Drill Hall, Leeds, October 9 to 15, 1906', November 1906, p. 398) noted that the the firm's 'merits are widely appreciated by architects and builders, and it is having a largely-increased sale year by year'.

6. Ibid. An advertisement for 1907, also run in *JDA*, bills the firm as 'sole agents for the Decorating Trade: Paripan is perfection'.

7. 'The Ideal Homes Exhibition', *JDA*, May 1910, p. 175. The brand name was still styled as 'Wal-Pa-Mur' on a Sanderson stand and by the press in December 1913. Playing cards were issued in 1914 to promote the change to 'Walpamur', and as a means of additional advertising.

8. 'Paint: The Walpamur Company Ltd.', *WPM: The pattern of a great organization* (Manchester: The WPM Ltd), 1949, unpaginated; the crown was adopted as the trademark of the WPM from Wylie & Lockhead of Glasgow, whose merchanting operation formed the core for that of the WPM its early years. The brand, Crown, seems to have been used first for the Walpamur subsidiary established in 1928 in Montreal. In 1933 the Walpamur Company (Ireland) was formed in Dublin. Between 1968 and 2008, through a series of corporate and management buy-outs involving AzkoNobel, Courtaulds, International Paints and ICI, among others, the two brands were separated. Crown Paints Ltd is still based at Darwen, at the old Walpamur factory, while the Walpamur brand is part of Orica Australia's family of paints, which includes Dulux.

9. 'Exhibition of Manufactures, Chester, 1912', *JDA*, November 1912, p. 405.

10. 'The Building Exhibition, 1913', *JDA*, May 1913, p. 195.

11. 'The Wall-paper News: A Review of the Wall-papers of 1911', *JDA*, February 1911, pp. 57–59.

12. The term 'Mecca' was used on several occasions, for example, 'Arthur Sanderson and Sons, Ltd', *JDA*, February 1908, p. 66, and 'The Wall-paper News: A Review of the Leading Sets in 1913', *JDA*, February 1913, p. 71; the 'drift of things' appeared in 'The Exhibition of Decorative Arts and Manufactures', *JDA*, November 1908, p. 401.

13. *Sanderson Minute Book: 1915–21*, 30 April 1915, p. 187.

14. 'The Wall-paper News: A Review of the Leading Sets in 1913', *JDA*, February 1913, p. 72.

15. *Sanderson Minute Book: 1915–21*, 24 February 1919, p. 74.

16. 'The Exhibition of Decorative Arts and Manufactures', *JDA*, November 1908, p. 401.

17. 'The XIII Annual Exhibition, Drill Hall, Leeds, October 9 to 15, 1906', *JDA*, November 1906 p. 398.

18. 'Exhibition of Manufactures, Newcastle-on-Tyne, October 4th, 1910', *JDA*, November 1910, p. 385; the screens were 10 ft x 3 ft and were featured again in 1911.

19. 'Exhibition of Manufactures, Chester, 1912', *JDA*, November 1912, p. 405.

20. 'The Wall-paper News: A Review of the Leading Sets in 1913', *JDA*, February 1913, p. 71.

21. 'Exhibition of Manufactures, Chester, 1912', *JDA*, November 1912, p. 405.

22. 'Manufacturers' Exhibits' [at the Franco-British Exhibition], *JDA*, July 1908, p. 231.

23. 'The Wall-paper News: A Review of the Sets for 1909', *JDA*, February 1909, p. 71.

24. 'The Wall-paper News: Messrs. Arthur Sanderson and Sons, Ltd, Berners Street, London', *JDA*, January 1910, p. 29.

25. 'The Wall-paper News: A Review of the Wall-papers of 1911', *JDA*, February 1911, pp. 57–59.

26. 'Exhibition of Manufactures', *JDA*, November 1911, p. 407.

27. 'The Wall-paper News: A Review of the Leading Sets in 1913', *JDA*, February 1913, p. 71.

28. See, for example, Art-Ko-Na advertisement, *The Craftsman*, vol. 18, April–September 1910, p. 287.

29. Patent no. 16,451, applied for 17 July and accepted 28 November 1911.

30. 'The Wall-paper News: A Review of the Leading Sets in 1913', *JDA*, February 1913, p. 72.

31. The first Sanderson advertisement promoting fast to light pigments was placed in *The Studio*, January 1914.

32. 'The Wall-paper News: A Review of the Sets for 1909', *JDA*, February 1909, p. 71; and 'Building Exhibition, Olympia' (special supplement), *JDA*, May 1911 p. 183; black carpeting was also used on the stand.

33. 'The Exhibition of Decorative Art and Manufactures', *JDA*, November 1908, p. 401, but chequer borders also appear in 'The Wall-paper News: Some Leading Designs in 1909', *JDA*, January 1909, p. 32 ('The "Chequers" Decoration', which was also shown in 'Exhibition of Manufactures, Newcastle-on-Tyne, October 4th, 1910', *JDA*, November 1910, p. 385) noting that it 'can be broken up with cross-panels at will, and the decoration quite suffices to enrich a room.'

34. See Mary Schoeser, 'Omega Textiles: A sea-change into something rich and strange', in Alexandra Gerstein (ed.) *Beyond Bloomsbury: The Omega Workshops, 1913–19* (London: Fontanka, 2009), pp. 17–25. Fry himself coined the term 'post-impressionist'.

35. 'The Ideal Homes Exhibition, Olympia, October 9th–25th', *JDA*, December 1913, p. 458.

36. This factory, in Ivrey, is now owned by Turquetil.

37. 'Duke of York at Chiswick. Visit Yesterday to Messrs. Sanderson's', *The Chiswick Times*, 28 March 1924, p. 5.

38. See Woods, pp. 32–34.

39. Woods, p. 14. John Sanderson was pronounced unfit for action at the end of 1914 and committed suicide as a result.

## Chapter 6: *Towards 'Wallpaper Decoration'*

1. 'Decoration from the woman's viewpoint', *JDA*, April 1931, pp. 117–18.

2. Although the marble papers were described as washable in 1926, it was not until 1931 that Sanderson Washable Papers were introduced, having an impenetrable surface that allowed ink, grease and nicotine stains to be removed with soap and water.

3. 'The World of Wallpaper: Wallpapers in 1927 (continued). More Manufacturers' Sets. A. Sanderson & Sons Branch. The Wall Paper Manufacturers Ltd.', *JDA*, October 1926, p. 323 (also noting handmade cut-out mica borders for use on ceilings) and 'The Perivale Set', October 1930, p. 350.

4. 'The New Sanderson Mill at Perivale', *JDA*, October 1930, pp. 342–43.

5. Ibid. It was the fire at Chiswick, which necessitated putting work out to other WPM mills, that spread Sanderson technologies (with the exception of photogravure, which was not widespread until the 1970s). The fire also harmed Sanderson trade to the point where, in 1929, the WPM took over the Berners Street operation.

6. 'The World of Wallpaper: The Perivale Set', *JDA*, October 1931, p. 313 and 'The World of Wallpaper: Arthur Sanderson & Sons, Ltd', *JDA*, January 1932, p. 17.

7. 'Wallpapers in 1936', *JDA*, January 1936, p. 18 and 'Perivale Papers in 1939', October 1938, p. 312.

8. 'The Exhibition', *JDA*, November 1921, p. 351; the stand is illustrated on p. 356.

9. This exhibition was in the spring of 1921; cretonnes had been included with papers at the Ideal Home Exhibition in March 1920, but the Uxbridge factory was not fully operational until autumn of 1921, in anticipation of which promotion of the Eton Rural range was intensified.

10. 'The World of Wallpaper: Wallpaper at the Ideal Homes Exhibition', *JDA*, April 1922, p. 142.

11. Ibid. The firm also exhibited at the Building Trades Exhibition only some weeks before the Ideal Home Exhibition. In 1924 a main feature in its stand was 'Earl of Onslow', a design reproduced in miniature in the bedroom of the Queen's Doll's House made for the British Empire Exhibition at Wembley in the same year.

12. 'Ideal Homes Exhibition: Some Advance Notes', *JDA*, April 1931, p. 127; the Olympia stand of 1936 even contained a marble bathroom (illustrated in 'Ideal Homes Exhibition', *JDA*, May 1936, p. 150). Herbert Jamieson was noted as the stand designer in 1910; he was a senior sales representative of the firm and his assistants included Mr. W. Pyke and Mr. Templeman.

13. 'An Innovation at Sanderson's', *JDA*, April 1932, p. 121.

14. 'The World of Wallpaper: A. Sanderson and Sons, Ltd.', *JDA*, January 1931, p. 13. Cut-outs also allowed for the indiviualised placement of animals in the 'Noah's Ark' frieze of 1932, a redrawing of another of Hassall's pre-war designs; see 'The World of Wallpaper: Arthur Sanderson & Sons, Ltd', *JDA*, January 1932, pp. 17–18.

15. At the factory 'the Duke recognised a lad named Rudolph, who last year spent some time at the camp for working and public schoolboys, which the Duke inaugurated and takes so personal an interest in'. 'Duke of York at Chiswick. Visit Yesterday to Messrs. Sanderson's', *The Chiswick Times*, 28 March 1924, p. 5. During his visit the Duke was shown a paper embellished with 'GRI', which had been chosen by Edward VII for Windsor Castle, as well as a 'paper destined to find a place in one of the Royal residences,' probably the paper ordered in 1923 by the Queen for the Blue Drawing Room at Buckingham Palace. 'The paper was an embossed linen ground in light camel colour and gold, with an Italian damask design in medium blue, triple flocked in wool, with a final flocking in pale Cambridge blue silk. This was the first time the room had been papered, as it had previously been hung with silk. Richard Jack, RA, was commanded to paint a picture of this room, and his painting, called *The Blue Drawing Room*, was hung in the Academy Exhibition…'. From 'A. Sanderson & Sons Branch, Perivale, Middlesex', *WPM: The pattern of a great organization* (Manchester: WPM Ltd, 1949), unpaginated, where note is also made of the Duke of Kent's visit to Perivale in 1933. These quoted accounts are based on previously published reviews sourced from historical journals, gazettes and newspapers. The painting is dated 1927.

16. 'Perivale Papers in 1939', *JDA*, October 1938, p. 314; the Disney animated film was released earlier in the same year. Sections of the 'Mickey Mouse' wallpaper border and frieze of 1930 are illustrated in Gill Saunders, *Wallpaper in Interior Decoration* (New York: Watson-Guptill Publications, 2002), p. 138.

17. Advertisement in *Punch*, 23 October 1938, p. iii, noting that the Sanderson Indecolor range included cretonne, linen and linen union, glazed chintz 'and the new lustrous finish washable chintz, called "Sanderlin", all *guaranteed* sunresisting and washproof.' The fabrics sold for 1*s.*11*d.* upwards (about £4.50 in today's values) per yard. For discussion of a nursery fabric designed for 1938 by Eric Gilboy (in the

Uxbridge studio from 1933–39) and a best-seller between 1949–54, during which time just one of its colourways sold over 40,000 yards, see Gawne, pp. 14–16.

18. 'The World of Wallpapers: The Perivale Set', *JDA*, October 1931, p. 313. In 1929 *Punch* carried an 'Ask for the Sanderson Wallpaper Book' advertisement with a storyline concerning 'the woman of the house' (13 February 1929, p. xi).

19. Gawne, p. 14.

20. *Sanderson Board Minutes 1931–1934*, pp. 1 (31 December 1930) and 12 (28 July 1931); this was a response to an 8.2 per cent decrease in Berners Street sales in the four months ending 31 December 1930. Having had its desired effect by early 1932, the budget began to be reduced, and was down to £2,600 by 1936 (p. 35).

21. 'The World of Wallpaper: A. Sanderson & Sons, Ltd.', *JDA*, January 1924, p. 27.

22. 'The World of Wallpaper: Arthur Sanderson and Sons, Ltd.', *JDA*, February 1935, p. 50 and 'The World of Wallpaper: A Sanderson Booklet', *JDA*, March 1924, p. 96.

23. 'Completing the Scheme', *JDA*, January 1939, p. 59. This report noted that lay visitors most often commented on the 'fresh and original' room schemes because they presented decor 'with which one could live'.

24. 'Decorators' Exhibition at Brighton: Some Attractive Exhibits', *JDA*, October 1937, p. 337.

25. 'The Building Trade Exhibition: Painters' Materials and Equipment at Olympia', *JDA*, May 1921, p. 166.

26. 'The Exhibition', *JDA*, November 1921, p. 351.

27. 'Among the Manufacturers', *JDA*, June 1922, p. 211.

28. The Uxbridge factory was extended in 1931 and, following successful experiments in shadow printing, a further 15,000 square feet were added, housing 30" and 50" automatic looms. In the meantime these cloths were woven by an outside manufacturer, possibly Simpson & Godlee in Manchester, who were known for shadow prints at this time.

29. Among the modern papers was 'Finella' by Raymond McGrath, for the studios he designed for the BBC Broadcasting House, London, in 1932.

30. 'Wallpapers in 1936', *JDA*, January 1936, p. 18; in the previous year it was noted that many fillings expressed the 'modern feeling for "horizontalism",' meaning the designs themselves, rather than the method of hanging ('The World of Wallpaper: Arthur Sanderson and Sons, Ltd.', *JDA*, February 1935, p. 50).

31. 'Press Day at Sanderson's', *JDA*, March 1936, p. 86, a record of a press day at Berners Street, something reported as if a Sanderson innovation.

32. The data on designers, taken from *Sanderson Wages Books*, was compiled by Eleanor Gawne, 7 December 1992.

33. The Haward Studio was founded in the early twentieth century by Sidney Haward and carried on in the 1920s and 1930s by Eric and then James Haward; the studio's designs for Sanderson included a hunting scene, introduced in 1929 and in the range on cloth until 1968, and produced as a paper for the American market from 1956; it was also revived in the 1980s.

34. See H. G. Hayes Marshall, *British Textile Designers Today* (Leigh-on-Sea: F. Lewis, 1939), pp. 161–64.

35. 'The Building Trade Exhibition: Painters' Materials and Equipment at Olympia', *JDA*, May 1921, p. 166. Berners Street held sole agency for the Easilit.

36. 'The Exhibition', *JDA*, November 1923, p. 375. Berners Street also held sole agency for the product.

37. 'A. Sanderson & Sons, Ltd', *JDA*, May 1928, p. 162.

38. 'Decorators' Exhibition at Brighton: Some Attractive Exhibits', *JDA*, October 1937, p. 339.

39. *RSA Minutes*, vol. 34, p. 34; this information courtesy of Phoebe Fox-Bekerman; see *Journal of the Royal Society of Arts*, vol. 82, no. 4232, pp. 183–99, for a lecture by Harold on 'Art Schools and Art in Industry', given on 13 December 1933. Harold's grandfather, Arthur, had also been a fellow, from 1875.

## Chapter 7: *Fresh Ideas, New Colours and Modern Designs*

1. *Architectural Review*, cited in Woods, p. 50.

2. 'Summary of the Annual Report of the Wallpaper Makers' Industrial Council', *JDA*, November 1947, p. 42. To help with paper shortages Sanderson issued an advertisement urging an improvement in the rate of wastepaper collection, under the banner 'Waste Not Wastepaper, Want Not Wallpaper'. See, for example, *JDA*, January 1948, p. 41.

3. 'Wallpaper and the Purchase Tax', *JDA*, December 1945, p. 54; this report asserted that just prior to the war 90–95 per cent of houses in Britain contained wallpaper and that consumption had been the equivalent of 15 million rooms per annum. In 1973 the UK joined the European Union and replaced the existing Sales Tax with VAT.

4. Patience Gray 'Centenary Fabrics and Wallpapers', *Design*, no. 136, April 1960, p. 39.

5. Advertisements in *JDA*, July 1941 and August 1941.

6. *JDA*, January 1941, p. 26.

7. 'New Sanderson Patterns', *Design*, no. 61, January 1954, p. 7.

8. *Exhibition of Historical & British Wallpapers* (Suffolk Galleries: Central Institute of Art and Design on Behalf of the Wallpaper Industry, 1945) (exhibition catalogue). Sanderson lent nineteenth-century hand-printed designs by Walter Crane, Lewis F. Day and Voysey, together with Watkins Wild's 'Hunting Frieze', Louis Stahl's 'The Peacock' and Panel 8 from 'The Phoenix Decoration' by W. G. Francis and E. V. Brand; within the text there was also the promise of the reintroduction of popular childrens' papers, 'right up to the modern Mickey Mouse and other Walt Disney designs' (p. 28).

9. The term 'contemporary' was applied to this style by 1937; see 'Perivale Papers for 1938', *JDA*, October 1937, p. 322. Morris textiles were not yet produced by Sanderson; the blocks were acquired by Stead McAlpin in Carlisle and used to print for many firms, the first of which was probably The Old Bleach Linen Co., Randalstown, in 1953, followed by Liberty of London and Warner & Sons by 1956–58.

10. See Mary Schoeser, 'Fabrics for Everyman and for the Elite', in P. J. Maguire and J. M. Woodham (eds), *Design and Popular Politics in Postwar Britain* (Leicester: Leicester University Press, 1997); and Mary Schoeser, 'Forty Years of Change…', in Penny Sparke (ed.), *Did Britain Make It?* (London: Design Council, 1986). The Sanderson contribution included a small all-over pattern of foliate diamonds, spots and dots that, in black on a bright yellow ground, had also been shown at the Suffolk Galleries the year before.

11. *JDA*, May 1946, p. 28; the *Daily Herald* exhibition was held in Dorland Hall, Regent Street and the Sanderson display included cut-out chairs of various periods in front of appropriate papers.

12. Sanderson advertisement in *JDA*, January 1946, p. 35.

13. The first flocking machine had been developed by Harold Sanderson in 1926, but was not successful until 1935. Further improvements were made in the immediate post-war period.

14. The crêpe-paper production continued until 1960. Screen-printing, introduced in 1934, was primarily used for Post Office banners, military badges and other low-volume orders such as shops' special offers.

15. Notley was taken over by Saatchi & Saatchi in 1972–73, but no records were transferred to the new owners at that time.

16. Woods, p. 46.

17. See Robert Burstow, 'Domestic Sculpture', *Apollo Magazine*, 1

November 2008; http://www.apollomagazine.com/features/2536141/part_5/domesticsculpture.thtml. Sanderson also exhibited in this period at the Ideal Home Exhibitions from 1947 onwards.

18. Such exhibitions were equally important in continental Europe, the USA and elsewhere; see, for example, Hoskins, p. 215.

19. These courses continued into the early 1970s; a training programme had also been initiated in 1949 at Potters of Darwen, which, like Perivale, was still part of the WPM.

20. 'Pattern in the Plural', *Ideal Home*, April 1954, pp. 66–67; 'New Sanderson Patterns', *Design* no. 61, January 1954, pp. 7–10.

21. Paul Reilly, 'Tradition and Experiment', *Design*, no. 43, July 1952, p. 20; 'Miscellany' was launched in 1952 with 'Quadrille' and 'Palisade'; the remaining two designs were issued in 1953, together with 'Travelogue'. British Celanese commissioned the designs to promote their cellulose acetate, which was then by far the cheapest among man-made and synthetic fibres, and also less expensive than cotton and linen. 'Perpetua' was subsequently screen-printed on cotton for Sanderson at Stead McAlpin, in June 1954.

22. Company memoirs indicate that the scheme was run by P. H. Simpson, a designer who came from the Chiswick studio; the bursary remained in place until 1965 and Haines was wallpaper design manager from at least 1970 until 1982.

23. *Decorative Art: The Studio Yearbook*, vol. 47, 1957, p. 60; the introduction of ICI's Procion dyes from 1956 onwards was also instrumental in bringing vivid fast colours into textile ranges.

24. *Decorative Art: The Studio Yearbook*, vol. 46, 1956, p. 65.

25. Seventeen of these are illustrated in 'The Courtaulds-Sanderson Collection of Ancestral Fabrics', *Ambassador*, 2-1952, pp. 87–91.

26. In 1952 contemporary patterns amounted to 4 per cent of British wallpaper output, rising to 20 per cent by 1956 and 'a large proportion' by 1959; see Hoskins, p. 217.

27. A very similar design was created by Lindberg for Nordiska Kompaniet in 1947, and printed in Sweden by Ljungbergs Textiltryck; see Lesley Jackson, *20th Century Pattern Design* (London: Mitchell Beazley, 2002) p. 91 and endpapers.

28. 'The Wallpapers of Yesterday and Wallpapers Today', *Ambassador* 1-1955, p. 102 and 'New Textures on the Walls', 8-1955, pp. 50–53.

29. Ibid., p. 50. It adds that in addition to 'eleven lively colours' there was a neutral surface that could be painted or distempered to order; this product, said to have a 'shimmering, sun-lit look' from the natural gloss of the jute, is another that had been developed not long before the Second World War.

30. From an analysis of mid-1950s records at Company's House by Sue Kerry, with thanks for her provision of this information.

31. The second Royal Warrant was granted in 1951, naming Sanderson as purveyors of wallpapers and paints to George VI. It most probably arose from the production of a hand-printed double-flocked paper ordered in 1951 as a replacement of the Pugin design hung in the Robing Room of the House of Lords.

32. Woods, p. 46.

33. These showrooms and the building, by architects Slater & Uren, are fully described in Woods, pp. 50–52.

34. 'Designed for Display; Sanderson's Magnificent Headquarters', *Ambassador*, 4-1960, p. 59.

35. *Decorative Art in Modern Interiors 1961–62* (London: Studio Books, 1961), p. 81, which illustrates designs by Madge Nielson, George Todd, Gordon Cook and Denst & Soderland of the United States.

36. 'The Wall Paper Manufacturers Limited: A Year of Active Businesss; Previous Profit Record Substantially Exceeded', *Ambassador*, 1-1961, p. 112, reporting on the AGM of the WPM held on 30 November 1960. The same report also notes the acquisition of the Birge Company and its ownership of W. H. S. Lloyd, and net profits of £6,200,000.

## Chapter 8: *A New Concept in Co-ordination*

1. Reed Paper Group, in which the Daily Mirror Group was a substantial shareholder, merged with IPC to become Reed International. John Ould, who had been with Reed since the war, joined the financial division of the WPM, becoming finance director of the WPM Group and sitting on the board of Sanderson, Crown and Polycell. I am thankful for his recollections, given in a telephone interview on 4 June 2009, which have informed my understanding of this and other aspects of the history of Sanderson. For further information on the history and influence of the WPM, see 'The Industry', in the exhibition catalogue, *A Popular Art: British Wallpapers 1930–1950* (London: Middlesex Polytechnic, 1989), pp. 45–55.

2. Bill Sandford typescript, Gosport, 13 June 1978, p. 6. The principle reason for the Perivale closure was the high property tax in that location. This account is the basis of the technical information noted in this chapter.

3. Woods, p. 53; this account is the basis of much of the company history given in this chapter.

4. The clocks were made for Sanderson by Whiteoak Designs and were faced with Triad patterns.

5. The recipe was obtained from America; the brand was not registered as a Sanderson trademark until 1978. For this and other details given here and in later chapters I am grateful to Michael Parry.

6. Lee Taylor, quoted in *Campaign*, 3 December 1982. Taylor also restructured the company's approach to retail accounts and in the process closed 11,000 of the 13,260 accounts in existence in 1982, to replace these with fewer, more specialised retailers.

7. A Sanderson fent shop continued on the Ramsbottom site into the mid-1980s, when it was moved to Manchester; for further information on the Rose Bank Printworks see John Simpson, *The History of Edenfield & District* (Edenfield Local History Society: 2003). Edward Turnbull had purchased a dye-works, the hand-block printing unit and associated machinery in late 1968, when Sanderson began a rationalisation programme. Thereafter trading as Edward Turnbull & Co., subsequently Edward Turnbull & Co. Ltd (for UK trading) and Edward Turnbull & Son Ltd (for exports), today the firm manufactures in Thailand, maintains Turnbull Design Ltd (for design and UK and North American sales) and is known as Turnbull Thompson. I am grateful to to Michael Parry and Edward and Paul Turnbull for this and related information.

8. Sophie Campbell, 'Paper-chase around Britain', *The Telegraph*, 23 March 2007.

9. Hoskins, p. 222.

10. Edward Pond, 'The Wall Paper Manufacturers Limited, 1945–1971', unpaginated exhibition catalogue, Whitworth Art Gallery, February 1972, introduction.

11. Some papers cost as little as 6*s*.6*d*. and a few as much as 26*s*., or about the equivalent of £20.

12. One of Wollner's best-known students was Wolf Bauer.

13. Rosebank collections continued to be issued intermittently until the late 1990s.

14. 'Furnishings Bewitched', *Ambassador*, 4-1969, p. 37; another Albeck design for Sanderson, called 'The Secret Garden', was described in 'Furnishings in Motion', *Ambassador* 1-1970, p. 49 as 'a cleverly patterned cretonne with horizontal emphasis'.

15. 'Ambassador Interiors: Furnishing Fantasia', *Ambassador*, 7-1970, p. 71.

16. Pond, *op. cit.*, p. 4; this was the last Palladio collection and included designs by the Sanderson Studio as well as John Garnet, Natalie Gibson, Joyce Storey and John Wilkinson.

## Chapter 9: *'Whole Hoggers' on Chintz*

1. 'Arthur Sanderson and Sons, Ltd', *JDA*, February 1908, p. 66.

2. 'The Wall-paper News: A Review of the Leading Sets in 1913', *JDA*, February 1913, p. 71.

3. 'The Wall-paper News: A Review of the Wall-papers of 1911', *JDA*, February 1911, p. 58.

4. Alberto Riva, managing director, B & B Distribuzione S.r.l., in correspondence with the author, 19 May 2009.

5. 'Wallpaper Manufacturers, Ltd: Sanderson & Son Branch', *JDA* (special supplement), September 1905, p. 16.

6. *Sanderson Minute Book 1900–1915*, 31 May 1912–25 April 1913, pp. 128, 139 and 149. The cheapest papers sold at the equivalent of about £2 in today's money; the most costly at about £11.

7. The second trade edition does not have the wallpaper, but yellow cloth covers instead. For an image of the paper cover used in the first edition, see http://aesteteslament.blogspot.com/2009/05/whyisnt thisstillmadeedition8.html.

8. Sanderson currently offers the Spectrum range in five finishes: matt emulsion, soft sheen emulsion, water-based eggshell, eggshell and gloss. Shades of Sanderson, a range of 120 colours selected to complement the present range of fabrics and wallpapers, was introduced in 2009.

9. This exhibition was held in late 1935; see *Apollo Magazine*, vol. 22, no. 132, December 1935, which includes several articles on 'The Chinese Exhibition at Burlington House'. Chinese patterns had been fashionable since the First World War; the change was in the move away from coloured grounds to those that were very light or white.

10. 'Ideal Homes Exhibition', *JDA*, May 1936, p. 150, where this room set is illustrated, together with the 'China and Sycamore' room and 'The Marble Bathroom on the Sanderson Stand'.

11. 'Perivale Papers for 1938', *JDA*, October 1937, p. 323.

12. A 'Lloyd Screens' brochure of 1926 illustrates several Sanderson chintz papers, including 'The Kensington Screen', which employed three panels designed by Harry Watkins Wild between 1919 and 1921; these panels became part of 'The Phoenix Bird' Decoration, a scenic that in total comprised twelve panels with four identical extensions, with additions designed by Walter Francis in 1927; it was reissued in the 1950s. Another, 'The Peacock Screen', utilised Sanderson's 'The Cedar Tree', which even at this early stage was mistaken for 'The Peacock', a very similar pattern that won the Grand Prix and Gold Medal at the Franco–British Exhibition in 1908. 'The Cedar Tree' was first exhibited at the Ideal Home Exhibition in Spring 1910 and was still available in 1957, when it sold for 265*s.* per 24-yard piece. See Woods, pp. 19, 22 and 31.

13. 'The New Chintz Tradition', *Ambassador*, 5-1960, pp. 104 and 114.

14. See Linda Parry *William Morris Textiles* (London: Weidenfeld & Nicolson Avenel, 1983; repr. New Jersey: Crescent Books, 1995), p. 48 and illustrations pp. 147–72.

15. 'Sanderson's Wallpapers in 1938', *JDA*, January 1938, p. 11.

16. Woods, p. 49.

17. In 1984 there were three other designers at Uxbridge: Rosanna Turton, Fui Fui Ho Tang and Anne-Lise Fraser, and a colourist, Lynn Ormerod. Pat Smart and Will King, who had been with the firm since at least about 1960, were based at Perivale, where they had charge of the hand-block and screen-printed wallpapers.

18. 'Arthur Sanderson and Sons Limited: Specialist Scheme', setting out objectives for 1983 and 1984, tabled at an executive meeting, 26 November 1982, typescript, p. 1. The scheme, which was relaunched in 1997, aimed to secure 400 fabric retailers and 200 wallpaper and paint specialists.

19. The brand remains active under WestPoint, see martex.com.

20. For a summary of these trends see Schoeser in Hoskins, pp. 234 and 238–40.

20. Clare Deville, customer service manager, in correspondence with the author, 27 May 2009. During 1986 and 1987 the company had closed BST Silks, concentrating all weaving at Manor Mill (Dawes of Nelson). The curtain-making service in Bolton also was expanded and sewing operations were introduced for bedding; the fabric was printed at Uxbridge. The Bolton site itself, having been sold off separately by Reed International, was purchased back by Sanderson in 1987.

21. David Smallridge, Walker Greenbank Brands managing director, in correspondence with the author, 28 May 2009.

22. Alberto Riva, *op. cit.*

## Chapter 10: *Moving with the Times*

1. 'Sanderson Quality Policy', draft, 24 August 1999, p. 1.

2. Sanderson Contracts Division, 'Operating Company Focus: Arthur Sanderson and Sons Ltd', typescript fax 26 March 1997, quoting this passage without notation, pp. 7–8.

3. Designs from 'Earth and Air' remain in production today, as part of the Fresh Flowers collection.

4. His period with Sanderson is described as 'successfully implementing a turnaround and disposal plan'; see http://www.sorbicinternational.com/ files/14-August2008-ChangeofExecutiveDirector.pdf. Lee Taylor oversaw the sale of Uxbridge at the behest of Gamma and retired as CEO of Sanderson a few months later.

5. Kelly Parnell, sales support co-ordinator, in correspondence with the author, 13 May 2009.

6. Kevan Rosendale, technologist, in correspondence with the author, 13 May 2009.

7. In 1996 a deal with Marks & Spencer to design bed linen resulted in a licensing arrangement with Coats Viyella plc; 'Antique Rose', the biggest-selling Marks & Spencer design, was based on a Sanderson original and resulted in other products, such as gift boxes. For this and much of the detail regarding this period, I am grateful to David Walker and Michael Parry.

8. Alberto Riva, *op. cit.*

9. Clare Deville, customer service manager, in correspondence with the author, 27 May 2009.

10. Parry joined Sanderson in 1971 as an interior designer and consultant for the Contracts Division, four years later was in the Buying Division, styling all weaves, and by 1981 was design manager under George Lowe, becoming design director in 1988 and commercial director in 1996.

11. Sales of wovens increased by 41 per cent, wallpapers by 29 per cent and printed fabrics by 7 per cent; 'Chief Executive's Review', *Walker Greenbank plc Interim Report 2008*, p. 4.

12. The Sanderson block sets include 102 from Morris & Co., ranging from 'Daisy' of 1864 to 'Bird and Pomegranate' dating from 1926–27, and a further 240, from 'Ewan' by Owen Jones for Jeffrey & Co. to 'Damsel in Distress' by John Harbour for Sanderson, 1972.

13. For Jacobs see Dorinda Talbot, 'Finders Keepers', *Homes & Antiques*, January 2008, pp. 80–83. I am grateful to Rozanne Hawksley for pointing out this article.

14. Most of the other Sanderson weaves are produced by various mills in Italy, Belgium and France, while all of the embroideries are made in India, mostly at Mulberry, Ethnic Silks and Parry Murray.

15. The term 'document' refers to such purchases. Items still in the archive include *c.* 1800–1940 chintz fabrics, both English and French, purchased from Haines; *c.* 1720–1960 woven silks and velvets, mostly French and purchased from the Lyonnaise silk mill Maison Jarosson-Voley; and toiles, mostly French, dating from *c.* 1760–1940.

16. For further information about the donation of three-dimensional objects see Gawne, p. 13.

17. David Smallridge, *op. cit.*

The following items give a good overview of Sanderson and the general history of wallcoverings and textiles for interiors. The abbreviations are used in the notes, which provide an additional guide for further reading. See also the online reading guide on wallpaper provided by the Victoria and Albert Museum: http://www.vam.ac.uk/nal/guides/wallpapers/index.html

*Ambassador*
*The Ambassador: The British Export Magazine for Textiles and Fashion* (incorporating *International Textiles*), 1940–72 (established and edited by Hans Juda; acquired by Thomson Publications Ltd in 1961)

Gawne
Eleanor Gawne, 'The Design Archive, Arthur Sanderson & Sons Limited', *TEXT*, vol. 17, Spring 1992

Greysmith
Brenda Greysmith, *Wallpaper* (New York: Macmillan, 1976)

Hoskins
Lesley Hoskins (ed.), *The Papered Wall: The history, patterns and techniques of wallpaper*, new and expanded edition (London: Thames & Hudson, 2005)

*JDA*
*The Journal of Decorative Art and British Decorator* (Manchester, 1884–1954)

Oman
Charles C. Oman and Jean Hamilton, *Wallpapers: A history and illustrated catalogue of the collection in the Victoria and Albert Museum* (London: Sotheby Publications, 1982)

Nylander
Richard C. Nylander, Elizabeth Redmond and Penny J. Sander, *Wallpaper in New England* (Boston: Society for the Preservation of New England Antiquities, 1986)

Schoeser, Mary, *English and American Textiles from 1790 to the Present* (London: Thames & Hudson, 1989)

Sugden
Alan V. Sugden and John L. Edmonson, *History of English Wallpaper 1509–1914* (London: B. T. Batsford, 1925)

Teynac
Françoise Teynac, Pierre Nolot and Jean-Denis Vivien, *Wallpaper: A history* (London: Thames & Hudson, 1981)

Woods
Christine Woods (ed.), *Sanderson 1860–1985* (London: Arthur Sanderson & Sons Ltd, 1985)